# THE TWIN CONNECTION

*Cailin and Hannah*
LOESCH

***The Twin Connection***
Cailin and Hannah Loesch

ISBN: 9781939288769

Library of Congress Control Number: 2014947710

©2014 Cailin and Hannah Loesch.
All rights reserved.

No part of this book may be reproduced in any manner without written permission from the publisher except in the case of quotations in articles and reviews. All trademarks remain the property of their respective owners. Quote from *Forrest Gump* (Vintage Books, A Division of Random House, Inc.) ©Winston Groom, used by permission.

Cover Photo ©Ali Smith
Edited by Lisa Pliscou
Proofread by Karen Kibler

*Wyatt-MacKenzie Publishing*
DEADWOOD, OREGON

Wyatt-MacKenzie Publishing, Inc.
www.WyattMacKenzie.com
Contact us: info@wyattmackenzie.com

## Dedication
To Mom and Dad.

# Table of Contents

**Introduction** . . . . . . . . . . . . . . . . . . . . . . . . . . . . 10

In the Beginning . . . . . . . . . . . . . . . . . . . . . . . . . . . 16

**BABY PHOTO ALBUM** . . . . . . . . . . . . . . . . . . . . . 20

In This Together . . . . . . . . . . . . . . . . . . . . . . . . . . . 25

Two Peas In a Pod . . . . . . . . . . . . . . . . . . . . . . . . . 28

The Giggle Girls . . . . . . . . . . . . . . . . . . . . . . . . . . . 31

Twin Telepathy . . . . . . . . . . . . . . . . . . . . . . . . . . . 35

The Dream Team . . . . . . . . . . . . . . . . . . . . . . . . . 41

Identity Thief . . . . . . . . . . . . . . . . . . . . . . . . . . . . 46

Exact Exam Examples . . . . . . . . . . . . . . . . . . . . . . 52

Scary Similar . . . . . . . . . . . . . . . . . . . . . . . . . . . . . 57

The Shining Twins . . . . . . . . . . . . . . . . . . . . . . . . . 59

The Inevitable Question . . . . . . . . . . . . . . . . . . . . 66

Screens and Stages . . . . . . . . . . . . . . . . . . . . . . . . 70

Built-in Best Friend . . . . . . . . . . . . . . . . . . . . . . . . 85

Mirror Image . . . . . . . . . . . . . . . . . . . . . . . . . . . . 89

The Twinterviewers . . . . . . . . . . . . . . . . . . . . . . . . 96

The Scooter Twins . . . . . . . . . . . . . . . . . . . . . . . 102

Encourager . . . . . . . . . . . . . . . . . . . . . . . . . . . . 105

Being "The Twins" . . . . . . . . . . . . . . . . . . . . . . . . 109

"The Other One of You" .................. 111

Guilty from Birth ........................ 114

Sharing ................................. 116

The Academic Race ...................... 119

Package Deal ........................... 122

Stuck Like Glue ......................... 124

Looking Ahead ......................... 131

Apart and Alone ........................ 132

Two-lane Road ......................... 136

Growing Pains .......................... 140

Together . . . In Spirit .................... 148

**A Letter from the Authors** ............. 157

Acknowledgements ..................... 159

More on the Authors .................... 160

It's an interesting combination: having a great fear of being alone, and having a desperate need for solitude and the solitary experience. That's always been a tug of war for me.

*Jodie Foster*

## Introduction

*Before you read the story* of our tumultuous, ever-changing, laughter-infused lives as twins, let me fast-forward to an important moment in the writing of this book. Cailin and I were sitting on a bench at the mall, and had just finished the last chapter. Next to us was a woman who had been eyeing us for a while, but had been silent the entire time. Finally, she opened her mouth and asked a question that we have been answering since we were old enough to talk.

**"What's it like being twins?"**

We've heard these words spoken by everyone—from our dad's office workers, to grandparents with their grandkids, to people at the grocery store checkout, to our own classmates at school. It seems that no matter how young, old, or somewhere in between a person is, they never stop wondering what it would be like to coexist with someone who seemingly serves no purpose but to mirror their own life.

We were about to respond with our usual, "It's fun . . . most of the time." But suddenly we were both struck by a realization. It was people just like this nameless woman at the mall who were our inspiration for putting together these stories for others to read—which we hoped would provide a detailed, enlightening, and totally authentic answer to her question.

"Well, it's interesting . . ." I began. I paused for a moment, and then Cailin continued with a smile, "In fact, we could write an entire book about it."

*Hi, it's Hannah here!* My stories are on paper painted with yellow, coral, and magenta. I hope you enjoy them.

*And now it's Cailin!* My stories are on paper painted with blue, teal, and purple. Have fun!

# In the Beginning

*Whenever somebody asks me* about what it's like being a twin, it's not so easy to answer, because (a) I've never known anything different, and (b) there are just so many different facets of twinhood! Some of these facets are pretty deep—like the unwavering feeling that I am never alone. Others are more superficial. For example, because Cailin and I are identical twins, it's like having a 24/7 opportunity to play tricks on people. (Pretty cool, huh?) And in a very fundamental way, it's difficult to explain what it feels like to be a twin because I don't have any firsthand experience of what it feels like to *not* be a twin. I mean, think about it—I've literally been a twin since before I was born.

When Cailin and I decided to write this book, it seemed like the best place to start would be to describe what life was like for us when we were little. So we put a lot of thought into it. We sat around and reminisced for hours about the first few years of our lives, trying to remember how we felt about being twins.

What we came up with is this: we didn't feel anything at first. Neither of us can recall comparing ourselves to each other or even talking about how we looked the same. But—as twins often do—Cailin and I had a special language that nobody else could translate. People who knew us back then tell us that we always seemed to understand each other.

Our mom says that when I was a toddler, I would tell her that I never needed to learn how to open doors because Cailin knew how to. The thought that I very seriously said that is a little freaky to me today. Did I really think I'd never have to learn to do everyday things because my sister could do them? Did I really think I would be glued to her side my entire life? What *was* I thinking?

I do remember that preschool was kind of a big deal for us. Not only was it the first time we would be in an unknown place away from our parents for hours at a stretch, it was also the first time we'd be separated from each other in a significant way. Some days we went together, and some days we went by ourselves while the other twin stayed home. I don't remember the schedule exactly, but I have a vivid memory of dreading going by myself. I realize now that our parents separated us so that we would become more independent and have our own experiences. But my four-year-old mind didn't understand that.

I remember clinging to Mom's leg and being pulled away, and then crying as I was walked into the preschool room. Once I got there, I hid underneath a table until someone coaxed me out. I remember watching all the other kids running around, playing and learning the alphabet and things, while I just sat, feeling sad and lonely. I couldn't get past the idea of my sister not being there.

Speaking of "being there," I think that's a good way to help explain why Cailin and I are so close. Because our dad's job requires him to relocate often, we've moved at least every three years since we were born. While a lot of kids have lived in the same house, in the same town, with the same group of friends their whole lives, Cailin and I are constantly having to uproot ourselves, land in a completely new place, and basically start over. Just when we develop a group of friends that we really like and trust, we find ourselves somewhere else, in a strange house full of boxes. Once again, there we are in a different school,

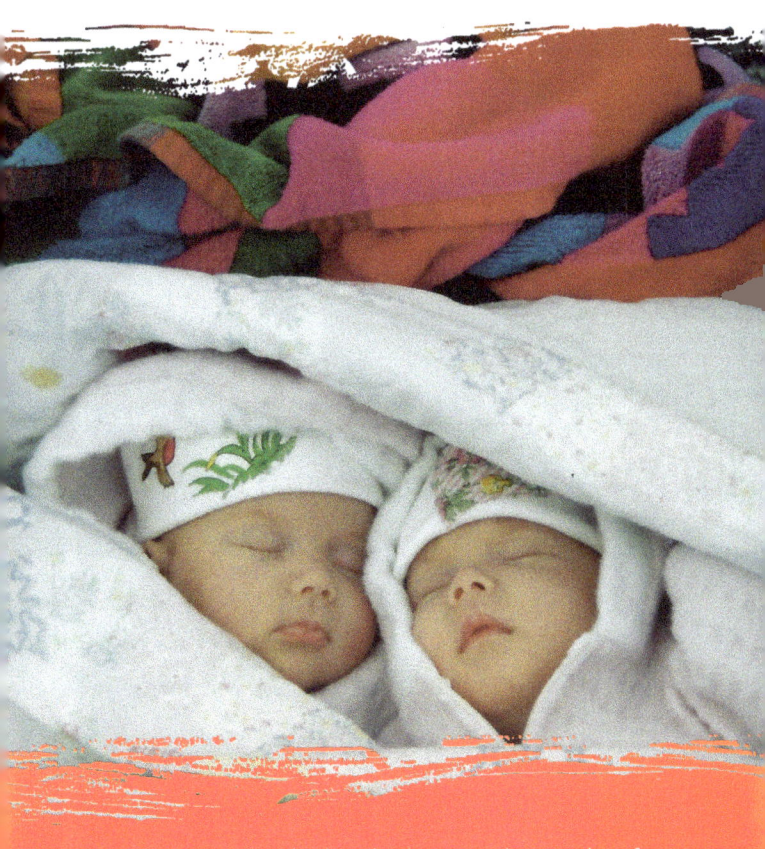

surrounded by hundreds, even thousands, of unfamiliar faces. Outsiders to that group of tight-knit classmates.

In a way, having each other is the only constant in our lives—we know that no matter where we move, we'll always have each other to brave it together. That's always been very comforting to me.

# Baby Photo Album

Here are photos of us when we were little.

## In This Together

*Fast forward to the summer* that Cailin and I were sixteen.

You know those unpredictable moments that make you think of something or someone from the past, and suddenly it's relevant all over again?

There are moments like these that happen from time to time that really make me realize all over again how lucky I am to be a twin. Well, actually, I always feel lucky, but sometimes I experience an overwhelming feeling of thankfulness, as if I just realized it for the first time.

Here's one of those moments.

I was in the car with Cailin and my dad. We'd just dropped off some friends after a long weekend together, and had begun the hour-and-a-half ride back to our house. It had been a busy weekend, and we had stayed up really late the night before at a concert. I could feel myself starting to fade into sleep.

Suddenly, my new favorite song came on the radio, and I snapped out of my daze. I'd been obsessed with it for months. Normally, when I find a new song that I like, I share it with Cailin, but I hadn't told her about this one yet. Not that I was opposed to the idea—it just hadn't come up. It was an old song, by an artist who isn't well-known these days. I was surprised they were even playing it on the radio.

About ten seconds into the song, I felt Cailin's eyes on me. It was dark, and I could only see the outline of her body, but I could tell that she was staring at me. "What?" I asked.

In reply, Cailin simply pointed to the car radio and made a heart shape with her fingers.

No way.

The one song that I never showed to my sister, by a now-obscure artist . . . how did she even know about it?

"Cailin!" I exclaimed. "This has been my favorite song for months now! You like it, too?"

"It's been *my* favorite song for months!" Cailin said with wide eyes.

As it turns out, we had both heard the song at the same time a few months before, because it was part of the soundtrack to a movie we watched together. After hearing it, we'd both jumped online, listened to it a bunch of times on YouTube, and then downloaded it, without knowing that the other was doing the exact same thing.

We spent almost the whole car ride home excitedly rambling on and on about the song, and I learned that we even liked it for the same reason: it was catchy, but oddly relaxing at the same time. I told Cailin about how I listened to it whenever I was nervous about something and needed to calm down and focus. And what do you know? She did, too!

It's little moments like this that really make being a twin worthwhile. It was such a small thing—a song that came on the radio—but it made me aware all over again that we are in this together. Awesome.

## Two Peas In a Pod

*I guess it's a concept* that might be hard to comprehend if you aren't a twin, but I truly can't imagine what it would feel like to experience life without my sister.

It's like Hannah and I are a team, a two-person alliance, the only two members of an exclusive club. Sometimes I'll get anxious about things, like taking tests or doing something for the first time; but in my mind, the situation is instantly made better the second I remember that Hannah is going through the exact same thing.

Our bond is so close, and it feels so natural to me, that sometimes when I go to friends' houses, I get an overwhelming feeling of discomfort. It has nothing to do with where they live, or their mom or dad; it's because I'm thinking about their siblings. Or the lack thereof.

We had a friend once who was an only child. After stepping into her house for the first time, my mind immediately began to race.

*Whose room does she run into after she wakes up? Who does she share clothes with?*

*Who takes on the other half of her chores? Who does she watch movies with when she can't have friends over? Who does she talk to all day? Who would she go to if she was having a problem with a family member or a friend?*

And it's not just kids without any siblings that I wonder about. One of our friends from middle school, Nicole, had a brother and two sisters, yet I was still in awe of the way that she lived.

*They might live in the same house,* I'd be thinking, *but they probably have different interests and maybe they even avoid each other as much as possible. I'm sure there are plenty of times where Danielle and Christina are at horseback-riding lessons while Peter is at football practice . . . Then what does Nicole do?*

Of course, people can be perfectly happy having non-twin siblings, or without any siblings at all. But it really goes to show how you just kind of get used to a situation that you've been in all your life, and things that would seem unusual to other people are normal to you.

Like Hannah said in the very first chapter— I've always been a twin. It would feel really weird to me to suddenly be an only child. Or to have other sisters or a brother. Similarly, I guarantee there are plenty of kids out there who would hate to have more, or fewer, siblings . . . and I bet there are only children who wouldn't appreciate always having a sibling in their way (particularly one *just like them*).

But the way I see it, we are all put in our family situations for a reason. Like, I know for a fact that if I didn't need Hannah in my life, I wouldn't have been born a twin. There is no other way to explain why some of us are born into a family of five, eight, or twelve children, while others go through the ups and downs of growing up alone. We all have our own personal needs and preferences, whether we're consciously aware of them or not. I've always held the belief that we can rest assured when it comes to things we can't change, that our lives are the way they are because that's how they are *supposed* to be.

## The Giggle Girls

**"Don't you two *ever* stop laughing?"**

*Something you should* know about Cailin and me is that we spend *a lot* of time laughing. We just do. Maybe we've got an overdeveloped sense of humor, but we just think laughing makes life more fun. We've always felt that way. In fact, we earned the nickname "The Giggle Girls" by our best friend's dad back in fourth grade—and that's after he observed us at the school bus stop for a mere fifteen minutes one morning.

You know how when you're with a group of your closest friends, everything suddenly gets a lot funnier? Like, something that would normally just make you smile, quickly becomes absolutely hysterical when you see your best friend rolling around on the floor cracking up?

As you've probably already gathered, Cailin and I have spent pretty much our entire lives together. We've seen the same things, met the same people, and shared the same experiences since the minute we were born.

I'm sure it won't be a shock to hear me say

that a lot of ridiculous things can happen in seventeen years. And because Cailin and I have the same sense of humor, every little thing that's even remotely funny always ends up turning into an inside joke of sorts. It's gotten to the point where it's hard to talk to somebody, *anybody*, for five minutes without them unknowingly referencing one of our little jokes. It's almost like knowing thousands of secret codes that can make us burst out laughing at just one innocent mention. And some of them are simply random—so you never know when you might find yourself face-to-face with a pair of laughing twins.

One of our favorite "Giggle Girls" stories happened on the Friday of Spirit Week at our high school. Everyone's expected to wear their class color. Freshmen wear brown, sophomores orange, juniors white, and seniors black.

Now, a long time ago, when we were in fifth grade, Cailin and I met this hilarious kid named Horace at Disneyland. Long story short, the three of us stood in line together at Space Mountain, and within minutes it felt like we'd known each other forever. We stayed in touch, and soon became good friends.

Horace told the *best* jokes. And he always

wore—on purpose!—big, oversized, bright orange T-shirts. Whenever I think of him, my mind just runs off into a flood of fun memories, and all I can do is laugh.

It may seem strange, but because of Horace, even the *mention* of a T-shirt has become an inside joke to Cailin and me. Whenever we hear the word, we always glance at each other and smile—and don't even get us started with the bright orange ones.

So, on this particular Friday, we had a substitute teacher in our geography class. He was wearing—wait for it—a bright orange T-shirt. As soon as I saw it I was immediately choking back a laugh. I looked over at Cailin, and could tell she was, too.

The substitute finished writing his name on the whiteboard, then turned to face the class. "How do you guys like my shirt?" he said. "I'm representing the sophomores today!"

That did it. Everybody else in the class was just acting like he had made a casual remark, but not Cailin and me. We were just about falling out of our seats with laughter.

The substitute glared at us. "What's so funny about my shirt?"

I know it was totally wrong of us, but that just made us laugh harder. If Cailin hadn't been there, I might have just chuckled to myself and that would have been the end of it. But whenever I felt myself start to calm down, I looked over and saw her laughing so hard that she wasn't even making a sound, her shoulders shaking up and down, and I would just start up again.

Finally, I could speak. "No, no, no—" I sputtered, "it's just . . . it's just . . ." And then I trailed off. It was impossible to explain. You had to be there. And the only person who really *was* there was Cailin, and she was still giggling uncontrollably.

Of course, the substitute geography teacher sure wasn't laughing. Everybody else in class thought we were crazy. But I love moments like these.

All I know is that there is no better feeling than to have somebody with your same sense of humor always laughing by your side.

## Twin Telepathy

**"So, can you read each other's minds?"**

*I can't even begin* to tell you how many times we've heard these words. Or how many times we've replied, wearily, "Uh . . . no."

One summer, when we were twelve, our Grammy Linda—who we were visiting in Tennessee—became about the millionth person to ask us the infamous Mind-Reading Question. We were in the middle of one of our trademarked Dirt Road Walks, where through the years Hannah, Grammy, and I have had some of our best conversations and made most of our Tennessee memories.

The second the question slipped from Grammy's mouth, I shot Hannah a penetrating glance, then paused for a second as ideas whirled around in my head. There was something about Grammy's excited face that in that moment acted as a barrier between my lips and the word "no." Calmly, carefully, I told Grammy what I could so clearly tell she wanted to hear.

"Yes, we can, actually! You need to give us a while to get into the proper mindset, though, or else it won't work."

As soon as we got back to Grammy's house, I grabbed Hannah by the hand and pulled her inside. After a frantic search for a room that lacked potentially skeptical family members, I settled on the only vacant room in the house: the bathroom. I shut the door in order to achieve absolute silence, then sat Hannah down on the rug next to me. This was *Operation Yes! Twins Can Read Minds!*, and I meant business. "I have an idea,"

I said to Hannah.

After a few minutes of rapid conversation, we got up and went to find our grandmother. "We're ready to show you our twin telepathy skills," I announced, and Grammy followed us out the door, no questions asked.

She knew that it was time for another Dirt Road Walk, and those are *always* interesting.

Once we reached the bottom of the driveway and began our adventure down the dusty path, I nudged Hannah, who quickly cleared her throat then looked over at Grammy.

"Think of three objects," Hannah told Grammy. "Any three will do. Then say them out loud. In her mind, Cailin will pick one. She'll whisper it to you, and I'll guess which one it is."

Grammy looked a little skeptical, but then she said, "Light bulb, lamp, window."

Now was the time! I dashed over to Grammy, whispered the magic word into her ear, then proceeded to burst into song and dance, skipping around the trail and singing "B! B! B! B!" at the top of my lungs.

As usual, Grammy didn't think twice about my little performance: she's totally used to my shenanigans. She just eyed Hannah with an inquiring, almost cynical expression. "So, Hannah, which object was Cailin thinking of?"

"Lamp," Hannah said promptly. "She's thinking of a lamp. It's so obvious."

Grammy looked shocked, and exploded into applause. Hannah was absolutely, 100% correct!

I breathed an inaudible sigh of relief. It was *working!*

Too interested to let us off the hook, Grammy declared the need for a round two, and came up with a fresh trio of random words.

"Mango, apple, cherry."

I whispered my choice into Grammy's ear, then continued to run around in circles while singing a song about a seemingly random letter of the alphabet.

"W! W! W!"

"Mango," Hannah said confidently. Once again, she was exactly right.

Our game went on like this for the rest of the afternoon. As we continued down the long dirt road on that long hot Tennessee day, we continued to correctly guess the word that the other twin whispered into our grandmother's ear each time. Grammy grew more and more delighted. It was true, then—we were twins who could

actually read each other's minds!

So are you wondering what our scheme was? All it was is the two of us knowing each other just a little too well. When Grammy had said "lamp," I started repeatedly singing "B" out loud. As Hannah and I had decided back at the house, "B" stood for "best," meaning Hannah was supposed to pick the "best" word on the list. How convenient for us that lamp was on that list, because the two of us have a *massive* inside joke about lamps (please don't ask, it's really just too hard to explain) . . . making it the obvious choice of the three objects. And what about the "W" rounds? "W" stood for "worst"—Hannah was supposed to choose the word that was the worst one of the three in the set. As soon as I heard our grandma name "mango" as one of the choices, I was about ready to do a victory fist pump into the air. That was an easy one! You see, Hannah and I have argued about which fruit is the best one in the world since elementary school. I've always tried to convince her that it's cherries, while she tirelessly insists that it's mangoes. Consequently, when she had to guess which fruit I considered the "worst," the obvious choice was mangoes.

That's why we guessed each other's word right every single time—we had some kind of experience or story or even a joke which made the decision clear as a bell.

Looking back, were we really fooling Grammy Linda? Heck, I don't know, but the look on her face sure made us think so!

## *The Dream Team*

**"Do you two ever have the same dreams?"**

*We were at the bank* depositing checks we had earned from an acting job when the question, which we knew all too well, slid from the bank teller's mouth. Hannah and I grinned, and I answered,

"Yes, we actually do! All the time!"

The teller looked surprised, and then laughed. He was handing us the receipts when our mom walked up. "Do you get to be a part of their dreams, too?" he asked her.

Mom looked a little confused. "Well, I get to watch . . ."

Hannah and I looked at each other and chuckled. Mom had assumed that the teller was talking about our acting goals—*those* "dreams," not our actual dreams! "Yeah, we have the same dreams!" I said, cluing her in. "While we're sleeping . . . then we find out when we wake up."

Mom got it. The three of us walked out laughing. And you know what the really great thing is? Unlike the Twin Telepathy gag, this time we weren't kidding. Hannah and I do have the same dreams—and we have for as long as I can remember.

There's nothing like the feeling of waking up and running into my sister's room, either crying or screaming or cracking up or just plain freaked out because of a very vivid dream I had, only to find that she had the exact same one.

I'll always remember the very first time the two of us had the same dream. It was a totally ridiculous dream, but I'll tell you if you promise not to laugh.

We were eight years old, and were going through this phase where we were absolutely obsessed with the movie *Jaws*. One night, after watching it for about the tenth time in a row, I went to bed feeling completely chilled to the bone at the thought of being attacked by a shark. While Hannah and I were brushing our teeth before heading off to the bedroom that we shared, I said something along the lines of "Wouldn't it be scary to swim in a pool with a shark?"

We both agreed that it would be terrifying.

Well, that night, I had the most bizarre dream. I mean, this dream was *weird*. It was set in this sketchy water park—complete with a wave pool three miles deep and sand surrounding the water on all sides—and was unusually dark. I was swimming around all by myself, when suddenly I spotted a tall tree on the shore, filled with dozens and dozens of big, juicy oranges! Being the Avid Fruit Fan that I am, I began to swim quickly through the waves, desperate to jump up and pull one from the branch. Once I finally had one in my possession, I sat down on the shore with my toes in the water and began to peel it.

Suddenly, a massive shark surfaced from the water. He was just floating by my feet, staring at me. Stunned at first, I felt like I was being stabbed by his large, beady eyes, and leaped onto my feet to begin my escape. I can recall running as fast as I could, too frightened to turn around to see if the shark was somehow following me. I woke up gasping, to see sunlight pouring into my room. I jumped out of bed and ran around looking for Hannah. She was in the kitchen, eating breakfast.

"Hannah! *Hannah!* I had the craziest dream! I was in this weird water park and there was sand and deep water and it was really dark and scary and there was an orange tree and you know I love oranges so I got out of the pool to get one and then when I sat down to eat it—"

"A giant, hungry shark appeared out of nowhere!" Hannah shrieked.

Oh my goodness, how did she *know* that?

"I had the exact same dream last night!" Hannah exclaimed.

We both looked at each other and just burst into laughter. I had no idea how it was possible that two brains could have the same dream, or why it seems to be so common with twins, but it sure was funny.

Since that day, we've had hundreds of the same dreams. You know the ones where you are being chased but can't run because your legs feel like lead? Well, whenever we both have one of those dreams, we describe the person who chased us to each other, most often discovering that he looked the same—hair, eyes, clothing. I shiver every time!

There was another time I had a nightmare about our golden retriever who was perfectly healthy at the time, but in my dream she suddenly passed away. Hannah and I both woke up that morning very upset, and I didn't even need to ask her why.

I could already tell she had the dream, too.

I mean, it's one thing to lead the same life in

the real world, but in our *dream* worlds, too? We just can't get away from each other!

## Identity Thief

> "So can you guys get away with switching classes?"

*During the first six years* of our lives as students, we never once tried the old switcheroo. There was just too much risk involved! Each time it so much as crossed my mind that maybe I might finally give it a try, I would be overwhelmed with a flood with horrifying images of getting caught, yelled at by the teacher, then sent to the principal's office. It just wasn't worth it. Yeah, you get the picture—I was one of *those* kids. For the longest time, I was sure that Hannah and I would never participate in one of the most Widely Known and Highly Celebrated Activities of Twinhood.

That all changed in the sixth grade.

I woke up one morning in the middle of September feeling on top of the world for no reason at all. It almost felt as if something important was destined to happen that day . . . I just wasn't sure what.

As I was tearing through my closet that morning looking for a skirt to wear to school, I noticed a pair of identical T-shirts hanging from a high rack behind my main set of shelves. I had never seen the shirts before in my life, and to be honest, they were making me a little nervous. They seemed to be staring me down. I could almost hear them calling out, demanding, "Wear us. Wear us and switch classes for once in your life. Don't be lame—do it."

Well, I couldn't let myself be intimidated by a pair of T-shirts, could I? I *had* to do it. So I went and got a stepstool, climbed on top, and ripped both shirts off their hangers. I stormed across the hall into Hannah's room and chucked one into her arms.

"Today, I'm in Mr. P.'s homeroom, and you're in Miss A.'s," I said firmly. "You'll finally get to meet my creative expressions teacher and I'll finally get to meet your gym coach. We'll even sit at each other's tables at lunch. We're doing this—it's now or never."

Hannah looked at me. Then she surprised me by saying, "Okay." Maybe she'd woken up feeling as daring as I had.

We went to my room and spent fifteen minutes digging through my drawers, looking for two pairs of jeans that were the same color and length. Bingo! Then we ran to Hannah's room in search of two identical sweaters. After that, it was into the bathroom for 20 minutes, making sure our hair was exactly the same, with each curl arranged just so on each of our shoulders. Suddenly I glanced at the clock and gasped. "We're almost late for the bus!"

We were running down the stairs when *Hannah* gasped. "Hey! It's Crazy Tie Day, remember?"

So we dashed back upstairs to our parents' room where we each quickly grabbed one of Dad's ties, ran downstairs, and bolted for the bus stop. We sat on the bus beaming at each other the whole way to school. It never even crossed our minds that we had made a tragic error.

Once we got to school, we each went to our own lockers.

Mistake #2.

Hannah and I went off in different directions. She went to *my* homeroom, and I went to hers. It was then, while I was standing in Mr. P.'s class reciting the Pledge of Allegiance, that my courage began to fail me. What the heck was I *doing*? I was in a cold sweat by the time Mr. P. began to take attendance. Realizing he was coming up on "L" names, I took a deep breath to avoid passing out. Then came the crucial moment. Mr. P.'s mouth began to open. His words still ring in my ears today.

"Hannah Loesch?"

Mr. P. didn't suspect a thing! My courage came roaring back and I raised my hand. Mr. P. moved on to the next name on the list. I was safe.

It was as if a huge weight had been lifted off my shoulders. Now, nothing could go wrong. I had engaged in a deceitful action that obstructed my identity and wasn't doubted for a second. I had falsely identified myself as Hannah Loesch and the teacher didn't even blink. It was all downhill from here.

I was still congratulating myself when my world came crashing down.

Mr. P. had come to a screeching halt. I darted my eyes to his, and was horrified to find that they were looking straight at me. It was probably only a few seconds that he gave me that awful look of complete and utter confusion, but it seemed like an eternity.

This was it. Busted. I was about to be

unmasked and declared a criminal, known by the whole school as the Girl Who Stole Her Sister's Identity. I was going to regret this for the rest of my life!

Suddenly, Mr. P. gave a loud, cheerful, echoing laugh.

"Oh boy, I see what you did, Cailin!" he exclaimed with a big smile on his face. "Switching classes . . . it's a twin thing, huh?"

I was so beyond baffled, I didn't even know what to say. How on *earth* had Mr. P. figured it out? We had done our hair exactly the same. We had worn the exact same jeans, T-shirts, and sweaters. No way. No way was this happening.

Mr. P. must have seen my expression of total bewilderment. "I saw you at your locker this morning," he explained. "You had on a blue tie. And now your tie is yellow. Nice try!"

As I dragged my feet back to my own homeroom, I met Hannah in the hallway, who was on the exact same walk of defeat.

Oh, for *crying out loud*.

"Tie?" I asked, and Hannah nodded. We both couldn't help but shake our heads and chuckle. We had spent all that time before school making sure that everything we wore was as identical as our faces, but in our mad dash for the bus we forgot to . . . coordinate our ties.

In that dramatic moment, I had no choice but to accept a conclusion that to this day I have still not been able to rinse from my otherwise peaceful mind.

The Hannah and Cailin Switching Classes Plan? FAILED.

## Exact Exam Examples

*One February morning* during my junior year of high school, I woke up with a sick feeling in my stomach and fog in my brain.

Usually weekend mornings are a positive experience, but that winter was an exception. Hannah and I were enrolled in an SAT prep class, and had to take practice exams every single weekend. So there I was, up at 5 AM on a Saturday and already running behind schedule.

Struggling to even get my mind going, I showed up at a random high school in our county with a handful of number-two pencils, a package of pepperoni and cheese crackers, and my sister. As I sat down in the desk that the proctor had pointed me to, I shot a glance behind me at Hannah, who threw a sarcastic thumbs-up sign in the air, laughed silently, then started filling in the bubbles that spelled out her name.

And there it was—the last time I looked at my sister until almost one o'clock that afternoon. I swear.

I've come to realize that standardized tests are pretty predictable. The very first thing you always find when you open up the test booklet is an essay question, and it always asks you to fill its three blank pages with an answer to some broad question, almost always philosophical, about life or friends or "the meaning of hard work." On this particular Saturday, the question was based on a simple quote about how "Everyone has the same 24 hours per day, but what counts is how you use it." The test-taker was supposed to explain whether or not s/he agreed that success should be measured in productivity only. To me, the answer was obvious.

My mind raced as I thought about all the people I've ever been inspired by. I thought of my parents, my Uncle Chief, my favorite actress, and my always-cheerful bus driver. But there were two names that really stood out to me as successful people I could write a great essay about: Gracie Gold, the teen figure skater who won the hearts of America during the 2014 winter Olympics in Sochi, and Grammy Ball, my grandmother who, at nearly 80 years old, is still out and about making people smile every day of her life.

My essay focused on the fact that Gracie Gold didn't even need to *win* gold to be the star of

the entire Olympics: the whole nation was so impressed that she was so motivated and hardworking at her young age that we as a country were proud of her no matter what color her medal was. And as for Grammy Ball? She could have never worked a day in her life and would still have been the most productive person I've ever known. She's always there for Hannah and me when we need her—and she lives hundreds of miles away. It's like she's got some kind of radar that flashes when someone needs her to cheer them up, and just like that, the phone rings. If I can one day be as influential as she is, I will die knowing that I lived my life to the fullest.

Once the essays had been collected, the class began work on the multiple choice questions. Out of the corner of my eye, I could see the proctor scanning feverishly over our responses, the gears turning inside his head. As I filled in hundreds of tiny bubbles, I kept wondering when he would get to mine. It was going to be the only part of the test read by an actual human being, and if nothing else, I was certain that he would find it original. After all, what other person would think to describe the most recent Olympic sensation *and* their grandmother?

Oh, wait. I'm a twin. I had another wild mind sitting a few desks behind me.

At the conclusion of the exam, while we were on our way out, I turned to Hannah, eager to talk about our plans for the afternoon. We were in the middle of a discussion about where to go for Sushi Saturday, when suddenly the proctor called out to all 20 members of the class:

"There appear to be two *very similar* responses to the essay question. I just want you all to know that if you cheat on the real SAT next month, your scores will be cancelled and you will be punished accordingly."

Hannah and I looked at each other and then kept walking. Of course it wasn't us. We opened our mouths to resume our sushi discussion when the proctor called out once again, this time clearly only to us:

"That means you, girls."

Hannah and I stopped dead in our tracks. I pulled her aside. "What did you write your essay about?" I demanded.

"That girl who was on the Olympics last night," Hannah replied. "And my second example was Grammy, and how she's always busy and everything but she always knows when to call when I'm—"

I interrupted Hannah with a maniacal laugh. She didn't even need me to say the words. She instantly knew that I had written the same exact thing. At first we were nervous about the fact that our thoughts are so alike that we can be accused of cheating even when we *didn't cheat*, but then we realized that you just can't worry about things like that. What can we say? It's a twin thing!

We laughed the whole way home.

## Scary Similar

*It was a Tuesday evening* in March, and Hannah, Dad, and I were out on a trip to the grocery store. We'd finished our shopping, and Dad was taking one last look at his list before we got in line to pay. Hannah and I stood there making jokes and laughing, entertaining ourselves while we waited for Dad. Nothing out of the ordinary, right? Well, apparently not everyone would agree.

It all started with a simple request.

"Hey, I forgot to pick up a gallon of milk," Dad said. "Could you two go grab one?"

"Sure," we said, and began to head over to the dairy aisle. Although we were wearing what I guess you could call "coordinating" outfits—each with a blue and white color scheme—we weren't matching. And we'd both curled our hair the day before for an audition we'd gone on, but mine was down while Hannah's was in a ponytail.

Suddenly, I heard a voice call out to no one in particular. It came not from a small child who hadn't learned to filter his or her comments, but from a grown woman. Giggling and squealing, she backed into a wall near where we were standing. She gave us a wide-eyed look as if she was both terrified and amused by something.

"Ewwwwww! They're creepy!" she called. I glanced around, but didn't see anything unusual. No rats, no cockroaches—not even ants. I was totally confused. I looked over at Hannah, who seemed upset about something. What did she know that I didn't?

Suddenly, in a sickening flash, it hit me. The woman was talking about *us!*

I wanted to crawl underneath the nearest shelf and disappear. I hadn't ever thought of us as creepy. Yes, we're two people who look and sound exactly alike—a concept that we both admit is a little unusual—but how does that make it acceptable to yell out anything that comes to mind the moment you lay eyes on us? I'm sure that woman understood that twins are human beings just like everyone else. I'm sure she was a nice lady who just wasn't thinking about how her words and actions would affect us. But I've never forgotten that day at the grocery store.

# The Shining Twins

*You've seen the movie*, haven't you? *The Shining*. It's an absolute classic, with one of the best horror scenes of all time. Young Danny Torrance is riding his tricycle down a deserted hotel hallway (cue the dramatically eerie music) when he suddenly turns a corner and sees two raggedy-looking identical girls, who wear matching blue dresses with pink ribbons positioned perfectly around their waists. The twins smile in a sinister way, suggesting in an airy and sickeningly sweet voice that Danny come and "play" with them . . . "forever and ever and ever."

For years now, Hannah and I have dressed up as the iconic Grady twins for Halloween. It's because of our costume choice that I find Halloween to be the most exhilarating holiday of them all. Every year on October 31st, Hannah and I are up at the crack of dawn preparing for the epic day ahead. Carefully, we lace up our baby-blue dresses and make sure the red food coloring is splattered on them just so. We paint our faces sheet-white, and use dozens of tiny brushes with patient care to color underneath our eyes with black paint until they appear bruised and beaten. We tousle our hair until it's perfectly unkempt, as if it hasn't been combed in days (or years!). As the sun begins to set, we slip on our Mary Janes—ones that are so heavy they actually slow us down and throw off our gaits—and head outside.

There was an unusual vibe in the air the Halloween that we were fourteen. I noticed just a bit of snow still left in the grass on the sides of the street from a blizzard that had recently hit our town. The trees were bare, and the sky was jet-black except for the yellow glow around the nearly full moon. It was a cold night—so cold that Hannah and I had actually considered putting on sweaters, despite the fact it would mess up the total effect. But we just couldn't do it. We decided to brave the night, and for the first time ever, hit the *town* in the traditional Grady garb.

Now, typically, our Halloween nights consist of traveling between neighborhoods in search of the elusive King-Sized Kit Kat Bar. But that year, and maybe it's because it was only two weeks after the incident in the grocery store, I felt like switching things up a bit. I wouldn't say I was motivated by anger, just a desire to play into the stereotypical Creepy Twin Hype while we had the chance to do it in a creative and deliberate way. I guess you could say that the woman in the grocery store had inspired me to take advantage of the fact that twins are often placed into the "creepy" stereotype. Why not turn a concept that had once upset me into an unforgettable Halloween?

Sometimes, I feel like there is an unspoken checklist that all twins must complete in order to fulfill their roles automatically assigned at birth, and it just so happens that dressing up as a couple of twin movie icons is near the top of that imaginary list. We let our dad in on our plan, and being the fun-loving guy he is, he agreed to take us to the local shopping center—which is filled with dozens of shoppers at any given moment. As we climbed out of the car, Dad sent us off with a few words of advice:

"Time to show this little town just how *creepy* you can be if you want to."

Hannah and I walked over to the raised curb next to the busy street that led into the shopping center. Where we were stationed, we could look down into the windows of the various cars and trucks.

We had an impeccable view of the faces of the drivers. Perfect.

I looked at Hannah, and she looked at me. "Here, like this," I said, and let my smile fade into a faint smirk. She nodded calmly, and stiffened her shoulders. I pulled her closer to me, so that our shoulders were barely touching. All simple actions, but necessary steps in our transformation from the Loesch twins to the Grady twins.

Finally, we were ready. And we stared at every single driver that went by, whether they were aware of it or not. Over and over again, our faces were illuminated by the headlights of the cars as they passed.

It wasn't long until we began to get reactions.

One man glanced at us out of the corner of his eye, but at first his expression didn't change at all. It wasn't until after he did a double take that he got a look of alarm on his face.

He drove away a little more quickly than he probably should have.

Our next victim was a young lady who was parked in the lot behind us. She was in the car with her friend, blaring music and singing at the top of her lungs. I tapped Hannah to signal that we needed to switch directions, and we steadily whirled around in unison until we were facing the car. The lady let out an ear-splitting scream the second her eyes met ours, pulling her friend in for a comforting hug. My sister and I kept our faces straight as she quickly turned on the engine and fled the parking lot, the two of us following the car with our eyes her whole way out.

But it was the incident that came next which ended our escapade at the shopping center. It wasn't that anything went wrong. In fact, it was just the opposite.

Something went very right. So right, actually, that we became so satisfied with ourselves that we didn't even feel the need to go on.

At this point in the evening, Hannah and I were deep into character. We no longer felt like ourselves at all, really—and we were getting so used to seeing horrified faces, we actually felt like monsters. Not only that, but it was getting so late that even this street—the busiest in town—was nearly empty. Only the occasional teenager would drive by, paying no attention to us at all.

It was then that a man pulled up and parked in the lot near where we were standing. He must've been about six and a half feet tall, and even just sitting in his car he appeared so powerful that it honestly wouldn't surprise me if he could lift a bus or something.

As we had all night, Hannah and I didn't break our stares. But it quickly became obvious that our scare tactics weren't working.

The man grinned and then he burst out laughing. Smiling ear to ear, he threw his head back and began to pound on his steering wheel. His response was so infectious that I felt a smile start to creep across my face, although I tried to stop myself by biting my lip and thinking about something else.

Hannah and I tried not to lose it—we really did—but it just wasn't going to happen. We turned to each other, and before we knew it were laughing right along with the guy in the car.

"What a *riot* you two are!" he howled through his open window. "I've never seen anything like this before!"

That did it. The next thing we knew, Hannah and I were rolling around in the grass, giggling hysterically, as the man lay draped on his dashboard, still chuckling like a madman. That went on for about five minutes before we finally bade our fan farewell and went our separate ways. Hannah and I went back to the family car and climbed in behind our dad, who greeted us with a high-five. Out of the corner of my eye, I caught a last glimpse of the man as he rolled down the road. I thought to myself that he was probably going to tell the story to his family once he returned home, and for that reason alone, our entire night had been well-spent in my eyes.

Heck yeah, we could be creepy if we wanted to. And on the last day of October? There's never a better time.

Best. Halloween. Ever.

## The Inevitable Question

*It was one* of those weird fall days.

Unless you live on a tropical island or something, you probably know what I'm talking about: one of those days in between Halloween and Thanksgiving, past sweater weather and carving pumpkins, but too early for holiday music and snow. Cailin and I have this thing where we strongly believe that as long as it's going to be cold enough outside to get frostbite, the *least* Mother Nature can do is make it snow.

But instead, we were stuck in the basement with nothing outside but a wind chill in the teens. Seriously? Brrrrrrrr.

So what else were Cailin and I to do but watch one of our favorite movies, *Forrest Gump*, for the billionth time?

I popped popcorn, Cailin made hot chocolate, and then we got comfy on the couch. We lay there, happily watching and barely moving, until we reached the scene where Lieutenant Dan meets Forrest and Bubba for the first time at the military base. If you don't happen to know *Forrest Gump* pretty much line for line like we do (yes, we're obsessed!), this is how it plays out:

> **Lieutenant Dan:** *Where are you boys from in the world?*
> **Forrest Gump/Bubba:** *Alabama, Sir!*
> **Lieutenant Dan:** *You twins?*
> **Forrest Gump:** *No, we are not relations, Sir.*

Suddenly, I lunged for the remote and slammed my hand over the pause button. Forrest Gump wasn't even a twin, for crying out loud, and he had just solved our Biggest Twin Problem! We'd seen the movie countless times already, and I'd never even noticed it!

"What are you doing?" Cailin asked, annoyed.

"Cailin! I have an idea."

I kid you not, we must have gotten asked that horrid Are You Twins Question at least four times a day our entire lives, and had never answered it any way but "Yes, we are." Leave it to Forrest Gump to inspire me to shake things up!

I spilled my plan to Cailin, and it was set. We just had to wait for the right time to carry it out.

As fate would have it, opportunity knocked that very evening, while we were standing in line at the pharmacy. I saw it coming the minute this lady got in line behind us. She slowly pushed her cart up and paused, looking us up and down. I know Cailin was thinking the same thing I was: *Any second now, she's going to say it.*

"Are you two twins?"

Bingo.

It took a lot of effort to keep a straight face, but we did it. And as seriously as we could, we answered, "No, we are not relations, Ma'am."

We must have said it pretty convincingly, because next thing we knew she was going on and on about how that was amazing because we looked so much alike, and that we surely must at least be sisters, and how far apart in age were we . . .

*It would have been easier to just say yes*, I thought.

We did end up telling her that we were just joking and had planned to give that answer to the next person who asked, and the three of us laughed so hard that the lady at the pharmacy counter couldn't help but smile, too.

To this day, Cailin and I are still asked upwards of four times a day if we are twins. If you are an identical twin, please know that we feel your pain. And if you are the one guilty of asking people who look and talk and act exactly alike *if they are twins*, just don't be surprised if they look you straight in the eye and solemnly reply:

"No, we are not relations."

## *Screens and Stages*

**"What's the best part about being twins?"**

*I've gotta say*, this is one of the most challenging twin questions we're asked. Why? Because there are *so many* Perks Of Twinhood.

Think about it. There is an incredible number of unique stories that can be told about a pair of identical twins. Remember *The Parent Trap*, where Hallie and Annie were separated at birth only to coincidentally reunite at summer camp years later? Or all of the great adventure flicks Mary-Kate and Ashley Olsen made when they were kids? And what about all those movies centered on the whole idea of the "evil twin"?

As Hollywood has demonstrated time and time again, twins are quite an interesting species.

I will always remember the day that Hannah and I decided to make up a crazy twin story of our own. After all, we reasoned, shouldn't we be taking full advantage of the fact that we'd been born doubles?

All we needed was a phone and some inspiration.

Now, if you are or ever were a teenager looking for a thrill at a sleepover with friends, you've made a prank call. What you might not know is that Hannah and I are Prank Call Veterans. As a matter of fact, one night at a New Year's Eve party, we made a prank call that changed the entire course of not only our eighth-grade year, but also our lives.

It was about one o'clock in the morning, and Hannah and I were hanging out in our basement with our best friend, Lob. Well, in all fairness, her *real* name is Megan. Lob is her nickname. Long story.

Anyway, by then the three of us had been up for almost an entire 24 hours, playing video games, eating pizza, and laughing nonstop. It was a New Year's tradition, and we were really going hard that year.

We were sprawled out on the floor in front of the TV, getting ready to crash, when suddenly Hannah made an announcement.

"Guys! I have a brilliant idea!"

Lob and I shot each other a look of curiosity, and then looked back at Hannah.

What on earth could she have possibly dreamed up this time?

"We should make a prank call. We could make up some kind of crazy story and tell it to anyone who'll listen."

And just like that, an idea was planted into my brain. I put aside the cherry lollipop I had been sucking on and began to divulge my plan to Hannah and Lob.

In a matter of minutes, I was sitting cross-legged on the carpet with Hannah, and Lob was perched in a nearby chair. I had a phone in my hand, and Lob had a notebook and a pen in her lap.

You couldn't tell yet, but we were no longer Hannah and Cailin. We were Mary Jane and Mary Jo, 87-year-old identical twin grandmothers from Georgia. Our hobbies included growing peaches, trying to figure out 21st-century technology, and watching daytime TV. Together, we had two grandkids: a nine-year-old boy who was always getting into trouble and a 45-year-old man who disliked his job and was angry at the world as a result. Lob's book was filled with notes that the three of us had written about Mary Jane and Mary Jo and their lives—just so we had something to refer to in order to make sure we were on the same page. We didn't want to accidentally stray from the "true" story of these twin old ladies.

Already, the premise we had come up with was more exciting to me than the tale of Chloe and Riley's British adventures in *Winning London* . . . and I loved that movie.

Soon, Mary Jane and Mary Jo were on the phone with the local Home Depot. In thick Southern accents, the two of us rambled on and on to Owen, the man who answered from the paint department, begging for decorating ideas so that we could get the house fixed up before our grandkids showed up for a visit. We provided in-depth descriptions of each grandkid, claiming that they would help Owen choose proper décor for their bedrooms. We referenced "polka-dotted paint," a product we had supposedly seen on *The Martha Stewart Show*, and asked to be connected to Martha Stewart herself when, in between laughs, Owen gently suggested that such an item couldn't possibly exist. We basically told Owen our entire made-up life stories, and even got him to tell us a little bit of his. It was abundantly clear from the very beginning that Owen knew that we were joking, but we were all having so much fun that he continued to go along with it. I figured that there probably weren't very many people calling the paint department on New Year's Eve, anyway.

Before he got off the line to begin his drive home from work, Owen let out a final laugh. "You made my night," he said. "That was fun." We thanked him for being a part of what had turned out to be an awesome New Year's Eve, and Hannah, Lob, and I drifted off to sleep.

The best part? Lob captured the highlights of the conversation with our video camera, and after letting Owen know where to find it, we uploaded the hilarious call to the internet for others to enjoy.

After only a few days, lots of people from school had seen the video. Students from all grade levels, some of whom I didn't even know, began to approach us in the hallways and recite the dialogue. How cool is that? I'd always join in and follow up with the line that came next.

After a week of our call being published online, the teacher in charge of the school's morning TV broadcast—Miss S.—had Hannah and me come to her office. With a big smile on her face, Miss S. told us how much she enjoyed the video, and asked if we would read the announcements as Mary Jane and Mary Jo the following morning. Hannah and I winced, and then looked at each other. We'd never done anything in front of our entire school before—well, not since the first-grade talent show, when we squeaked out a song from *The Saddle Club* and almost fainted trying.

Would we do it? Or were we going to tell Miss S. that we were too scared?

Suddenly, it occurred to me that life is too short to say no to things simply because you're afraid of what might happen. And that was all it took to change my mind.

The next morning, Hannah and I arrived at school wearing gray wigs and sporting matching canes, which we, for whatever reason, had laying around the house. We walked over to the TV room, sat down at the news desk, and positioned

ourselves in front of our packet of announcements. Then Mary Jane and Mary Jo proudly led the Pledge of Allegiance, squinted to read the weather report and list of upcoming school activities, and marveled at the Trivia of the Day, all interspersed with banter that could only come from a pair of identical-twin senior citizens who have more energy than all their grandkids combined. The second the cameras were off, I grinned at Hannah, who grinned right back.

Isn't it funny how nothing's really scary when you're not only with your favorite person in the world, but *also* pretending to be an 87-year-old lady from Georgia?

The second Hannah and I left the TV room and began sprinting to our first-period classes, people began to call out to us.

"Way to go, guys!" exclaimed a girl from our lunch period, and her best friend chimed in, "Nailed it." One boy flashed a smile and an enthusiastic thumbs-up sign as he headed to math class. And our German teacher, Frau M., said firmly, "You two need your own TV show."

*Since when do people say things like this to us?* I thought. I was used to hiding back in the shadows of other students who had long been known around the school for something: theater, sports, art . . . those kinds of things. It was like Hannah and I had suddenly become Active Members of the Student Body, and let me tell you, it felt *good!*

About a month later, our class was gearing up for the eighth-grade poetry slam. Now, bear in mind, this is not in any way something I ever had, or had ever planned on, participating in—not because I don't enjoy reading or writing poetry, but because I hadn't previously had the guts to do it. But this time we didn't really feel we had a choice, which, in retrospect, I am so thankful for.

It was a sunny Friday morning, and I was sitting with a few of my friends in my creative expressions class. Suddenly, the teacher, Miss T., called out to me from her desk across the room.

"Cailin, will you come here for a second, please?"

I swallowed hard. This was a repeat in history, it really was. Remember how I felt when Mr. P. was seconds away from calling me out for lying about my identity? This was that feeling, only with an intensified magnitude. I had an inkling that it had something to do with that darned prank call—and actually, as a result of that supposition, every butterfly that was trapped inside me just disappeared.

Since *when* was I totally comfortable getting attention like this?

Well, it turned out that I was right. Miss T. wanted Hannah and me to write a poem from the point of view of Mary Jane and Mary Jo, and perform it on the tiny little cafeteria stage during the poetry slam. Of course, with my new feeling of Twin Confidence, I said yes right then and there, before I even raised the idea to Hannah. After all, we'd be up there together, and we'd be playing the part of a couple of ladies six times our age.

How bad could it be?

That night, I told Hannah what I had agreed for us to do. She felt a little uneasy about it at first, but I reminded her that I would be right there with her, and she eventually gave me a look that I knew meant we were finally seeing eye to eye.

So now we had a mission to fulfill. The two of us spent hours really digging into the minds of a pair of twins in their late 80s. We started off our exploration by asking ourselves a few deep questions. What must it feel like for them to have spent their entire lives as twins? Did they always enjoy it, or were there rough times, too? How did their relationship change as they got older?

Believe it or not, Mary Jane and Mary Jo were actually getting me thinking about my own relationship with my twin. But I digress.

Eventually we decided that these areas of exploration were just too deep for the school poetry slam, so we went in a different direction. After a bit of brainstorming, Hannah and I scrawled out a poem about grandkids and their various activities. With a snappy rhyme scheme and jokes that were relatable to people of all ages and types, we finally felt ready for our next big challenge. We each printed off a copy of our poem and went to sleep.

*Grandkids, grandkids, they are so fine!*
*I'm so glad my grandkids are mine.*
*My, do they love their video games.*
*Especially my grandson, James . . .*

The next day was fabulous. I must admit, it was a little nerve-wracking, too, just because we were actually able to see the audience's reactions, which isn't possible when you're stuck in people's computers or on a TV screen. I even got tripped up and said the wrong line at one point, but it was okay because Hannah and I devised a self-rescue plan with just one look and were back on track in a millisecond.

The *really* great thing about the poetry slam? It was being able to leave my comfort zone, take a risk, and have fun entertaining others. Which is good, because I definitely needed that mindset to survive what was to come.

Eighth grade was drawing to an end, and our classmates were once again joining forces for a major production. The difference is, this time it was going to be in front of the entire school, not just the eighth grade.

Yes, it was time for the annual talent show.

I remember the day very clearly. We were sitting in homeroom when a voice came over the loudspeaker, announcing that there would be an audition for anyone looking to be the host of the talent show. Even though Hannah wasn't there, I could just sense that she was as excited as I was.

Minutes later, we met in the hallway.

"We're gonna do it," Hannah said.

I didn't even need to say anything—of *course* we were!

Turns out, we were both chosen as the hosts, which was basically a miracle for us. Sure, we had recently discovered our ability to get up and do things in front of a group of people, but doing it alone would have been an entirely different situation.

We were determined to do a really great job. In fact, I had a lightning bolt of inspiration, and I took it straight to the director of the show. My idea was unusual, but I believed in it and so did Hannah—and, to our surprise, so did every single person who was working so hard to make the talent show happen.

It was so on.

For the next few days, Hannah and I worked nonstop. We wrote pages and pages of dialogue. We took a trip to the local thrift shop, where we picked up two silky floor-length evening dresses and shiny pearl necklaces. We memorized our scripts and rehearsed like crazy.

Finally, it was the night of the Big Show, and we were ready.

Our entire family was over, including Grammy and Poppy Ball, who we hadn't seen in over a year. We all crammed ourselves into Dad's van on the ride over to the school, and we joked and laughed the whole way there—leaving no time for Hannah and me to feel even the least bit nervous. Finally, the car came to a halt, and for the first time all night I began to feel a tinge of apprehension in my stomach. Hannah and I stepped out and walked slowly, thoughtfully, to the auditorium, then backstage, leaving our family behind in their seats.

In the grand scheme of things, the show was such a small thing. But with our recent history of overcoming our fears and having a few triumphs as a result, it was almost as if the entire year was riding on our shoulders—everything came down to one night. I felt compelled to make it our best performance yet, with Mary Jane and Mary Jo funnier and wittier than ever, which made the stakes higher than they were before. Things had been going so well, the last thing I wanted was for us to mess up on the night of not only our biggest show, but our final one of the school year. My mind kind of went into a haze as the pressure began to build.

In that moment, I caught Hannah's eye, and I immediately could sense her worry as well. But just as quickly as I had detected it, the fear disappeared and the look on her face softened. Before I knew it, I no longer felt tense, either. It had just completely left us at the exact same time. Suddenly, I heard a loud, clear voice saying our names. Standing behind the curtain next to

Hannah, I checked to make sure my pearl necklace was positioned on the center of my chest and that my microphone was on. The lights dimmed except for a small spotlight which focused on the area front and center of the massive auditorium. I peered through a small crack in the curtain, catching a glimpse of a thousand pairs of eyes that were about to be focused on only Hannah and me. We took a deep breath.

Then Mary Jane and Mary Jo walked onto the stage.

We had on our gray wigs and glasses, and stood side by side in black flats that added not a centimeter of height to our 87-year-old statures. I began to speak, and right away, the auditorium filled with laughter. And I . . . relaxed.

The fun continued for hours, with Hannah and me coming and going from the stage, tossing out jokes and getting bigger reactions every time. After we had announced the last act and given our final commentary, the audience burst into a thundering applause as we pulled off our wigs and threw aside our canes.

As we ran down the steps that poured us into the sea of smiles and claps, I heard something that I have to this day not forgotten. The words came from Nate, a kid who was performing that evening.

"That's how you *do* it!"

And as my feet landed on the final step, perfectly in sync with Hannah's, it hit me: Nate was right, we *had* done it. We had an idea that started as a late-night phone call inspired by the hype surrounding identical twins, created some peculiar characters of our own, and eventually turned it into a show for an audience of thousands. Later, as Hannah and I watched Nate charm the audience with his soul singing, and Caitlyn captivate with her lyrical dancing, I kept thinking about how glad I was to not only be there to see them all, but be a part of the show myself for once. And the only reason we were bold enough to do it was that we were together, and we had each other for support at any given moment, no matter how the crowd was reacting.

We still make videos as Mary Jane and Mary Jo, and you can bet that next time they're asked to make an appearance somewhere, we'll be all for it. It's almost like they're a part of us now. And they actually brought Hannah and me even closer than we already were.

That's a really huge deal!

## Built-in Best Friend

*When we meet someone* new, often one of the first things Cailin and I are asked is:

**"So, do you two have the same friends?"**

No matter how many times I'm asked this question, I think for a while before speaking, but I always decide on the same, perfectly honest answer. "Well, yes, we actually do."

You know what I find very, very interesting? I go to school with quite a few sets of twins, but my sister and I are, from what I can tell, by far the closest to each other. I really do consider Cailin my best friend. I don't think every twin would say this about their sister or brother. We have the same sense of humor. We're interested in the same things. We're always together, pretty much without exception. Heck, even when we're sleeping, we have the same dreams! How can I call anyone else my best friend?

There's a girl in our German class who is also an identical twin. Just the other day, I asked her if she was in any of the same classes as her sister.

She said no, adding that she was glad, because her sister drives her crazy! From what I've noticed, she hangs out with a completely different group of friends than her sister does.

Not Cailin and me. The only time we've had different friends was when we were in different classes, but all it took was one time getting together after school for us all to become friends. Cailin and I were put in the same classes for second, seventh, tenth, and eleventh grade, the grade we are in now. We'll probably be in the same classes next year as well.

In elementary school, aside from second grade, we were specifically put in different classes for the same reason we were separated in preschool: so that we learned how to be independent, and so we had a chance to make friends other than each other.

Fourth grade was a memorable year for me. We were in different classes, and Cailin was with our best friend, Lob, while I was stuck in a classroom of people I didn't know. I was so busy feeling left out, I didn't even try to get to know people in my own class at first. The three of us would ride the bus together, walk into school together, and then I would turn left into my classroom and the two of them would turn right. Then, on the bus ride home, they would go on and on about all the hilarious things that happened in Miss M.'s class that day, laughing hysterically, and I wouldn't be able to join the conversation because I had no idea what they were talking about. That was hard, feeling so detached from our group of three.

Sometimes I still get that same anxious feeling of being left out. For example—and it may sound a little ridiculous—just a few weeks ago in English class, Cailin was put into a different group for a book discussion, and she sat across the room from me. Every few minutes, I would hear her laughing with her group, and I couldn't help but wonder what was so funny. It's almost like I have a need to know what's going on with her at all times, or I get anxious. I've talked to her about it, and she says she feels the same way. Though it may be hard sometimes, I guess missing my sister so easily just goes to show how important it is to me when she's there.

## Mirror Image

CASTING: IDENTICAL TWINS, AGES 16-45,
FOR NATIONAL COMMERCIAL.

*When Cailin and I saw* this as a subject line in our email inbox, we knew right away we had to go out for it. No matter what happened, we figured, it would mean a trip to New York City, and therefore the Times Square Jamba Juice—an occasion always welcomed by the two of us.

A few days later, we were sitting in a waiting room on the top of a New York City skyscraper, completely surrounded by twins. Everyone in the room was sitting next to somebody who looked just like them. Nobody was asking each other what it was like to be a twin, because everyone knew.

I had never seen so many pairs of twins in the same room in my life. Each pair was sitting side by side in chairs around the room and on the floor, wearing matching clothes and with their hair fixed exactly alike. Just as you'd expect from the casting call, their ages ranged from about a year younger than Cailin and me to about 30 years older.

The thing that really amazed me is that even though I hadn't spoken a word to any of them, I immediately felt like I could relate to them; like I understood them. Looking around from pair to pair, I noticed a pattern that absolutely fascinated me: each twin somehow matched their brother or sister sitting next to them. And I don't just mean clothes and hair—I mean their overall aura . . . their energy, their vibe—whatever you want to call it.

The sisters across from us were giggling and glancing back and forth at each other's phones, clearly sharing the same joy and feeding off of each other's upbeat attitude.

The two girls sitting next to us with the matching blonde ponytails and dark eye makeup were twirling sections of their long bangs around their fingers. It seemed to me that they were both nervous.

One of the boys in the corner appeared tired and exasperated, as if he had just walked across the entire state of New York to get to the audition that day. His brother must have taken the hike with him, because he didn't look much different.

I looked at my sister and wondered what our aura was. And then they called us in to audition.

That was right before Christmas. About a week later, on New Year's Eve, we got a call saying that Cailin and I had gotten the part, along with another pair of twins. I remember we were in the kitchen making pork and sauerkraut, our family's New Year's tradition and (amazingly) a symbol of good luck, when we heard the news. My sister and I hugged each other and agreed that it couldn't be a more exciting way to end the year.

The adventure officially began just days later, when we were back in New York City for our wardrobe fitting. While we were waiting to get measured, Cailin and I noticed a guy who looked to be in his 20s sitting a table away, digging through a backpack. I didn't recognize him from the audition, but then we were only there for a few minutes out of the two days of auditions total. He was sitting alone. After he finally found what he was looking for—a pack of gum—we invited him to join us.

His face lit up and he grabbed his backpack and pulled over a chair.

"I don't normally do this whole acting thing," he said. "My brother is the actor between the two of us. I'm Jeff, by the way."

Jeff went on to tell us that he was a full-time

police officer, and his twin brother, Sam, was a firefighter as well as an actor. But for this part, he explained, Sam wanted him to audition with him because it was a casting for twins. Now that they'd gotten the parts, Sam couldn't get the day off work for the fitting, so Jeff had to go alone.

"It's crazy," he added, laughing, "because I've never done anything like this before, and I'm the one who has to be here representing the two of us."

We talked and talked, mostly about what it was like being twins. Jeff told us all about what it was like for him and his brother as teenagers, and in many ways, it reminded me of my relationship with my sister.

I was having so much fun I actually didn't want to leave when they called Cailin and me back to try on clothes.

The Monday after the fitting was filming day. It also happened to be a record-breaking cold day in New York City, with a *high* that was below zero. The walk from our hotel to the set was only a block, not even long enough to take a cab, but the frigid temperature made it feel like miles. The whole way there, all I could think about was finding Sam and Jeff and seeing what they were like together. Were they as close to each other at

27 years old as Cailin and I were at 17? Did they still think alike? Did they still finish each other's sentences?

The actual commercial was being filmed in a tiny old-school burger joint, so they had to rent out a vacant nearby building to use during filming. This is where the cast went for hair and makeup, wardrobe, catering . . . and to just hang out when we weren't needed on set. That's where my sister and I were instructed to go when we first arrived.

I remember going down some stairs and walking down a long hall and finally turning a corner that led to the "cast holding room"—what a creepy term, huh?—and in about two seconds all of my questions were answered.

There they were, wearing matching jeans and gray T-shirts, leaning against a doorway. Both Sam and Jeff were holding their phones (matching cases, naturally) in their right hands, had their left hands in their left jeans pockets, and were standing with their left leg crossed slightly over their right. And, even more amazingly, both had the same expression on their faces, a Look Of Deep Concentration. Standing there, I literally felt like I was seeing double. Quickly I snapped a picture, which I still have on my phone to this day.

The day was full of Twin Talk. Huddling in our coats, Sam, Jeff, Cailin, and I sat at a card table, near what we were convinced was the building's only heat vent, and told story after story about our lives as twins. Yes, Sam and Jeff very clearly still thought alike. They still finished each other's sentences. They still laughed at the same time, and then when they stopped laughing, caught each other's eyes and started all over again.

In a way, this whole experience was very reassuring to me. I felt like I was getting a glimpse into what Cailin and I would be like in the future—and I was very happy with what I saw. I was glad to know that the bond my sister and I had wouldn't dissolve over time, just because we got older.

Eventually, Cailin and I got called down to set to film our parts in the commercial, and then when we were done, we got to watch Sam and Jeff film theirs. At the end of the day, Sam and Jeff high-fived Cailin and me. "Go team!" they yelled as we said our goodbyes and headed off in two different directions.

On the walk back to the hotel, the air felt even colder than it had on the way there, with the sun slowly sinking behind the skyscrapers.

But my heart felt warm.

# The Twinterviewers

*At the age of fourteen*, Hannah and I made the single best decision of our teenage lives. I am not kidding when I say that I think every day about how thankful I am for it.

The story starts on a sunny Monday afternoon. It was the kind of day that seemed to welcome a friendly game of some sort of a team sport. In fact, it just happened to be the moment that Hannah and I were walking to our very first lacrosse practice, despite the fact that we didn't even understand how the game *worked*. All we knew was that lacrosse seemed to be a popular sport among the other eighth-grade girls. And so there we were, heading down to the field with the rest of them.

But after only about three whistle blows, I was already dreading the sound of a fourth one. I didn't like having to run around with a stick that was too heavy for me to even hold over my head. I didn't like physically slamming into my teammates to try to snatch the ball. But mostly, I didn't like the nagging feeling that I should be somewhere else, doing something else. I put my stick over my shoulder, picked up my water bottle, and then walked over to the coach.

"This really is just not for me," I said. I will never forget her reaction—a terrifying mix of anger and disgust. But every part of me was confident that I had made the right choice, and deep down, I knew that nothing else should matter. In that moment of deep thought, I noticed Hannah in my field of peripheral vision. She seemed to be getting ready to make a move, and next thing I knew, we were on the grassy path back to the drawing board together.

*You can't spend dozens of hours per week doing something that you simply don't enjoy*, I thought to myself. And thankfully, I didn't have to, and neither did my sister. It was the car ride home from that very lacrosse practice that Hannah and I decided we wanted to be journalists.

You know that dream you've always had hanging out at the bottom of your heart, but have kept hidden with the antagonizing "more realistic" goal? That was always journalism for me. I was obsessed with watching news programs and talk shows, but it just didn't cross my mind that I would ever have the ability to be One Of The

People On Them. As Hannah and I sat in our bedrooms and filmed web videos on everything from random facts to science experiments, we dreamed of one day being a part of something bigger than we had the resources to create ourselves. And finally, we were ready to get the ball rolling.

Things started moving pretty fast from there. While looking online, Hannah came across a casting call for students looking to become reporters for *Teen Kids News*, an Emmy-winning news series for people our age. We decided to go for it together. But then a disaster hit: I got sick with the flu on the day of the audition in New York.

Suddenly, Hannah didn't have a partner in crime. She was furious at me, going on and on about how awful it was that whenever something bad happened to me, it dragged her down, too.

I got a brilliant idea. Video audition! As soon as I had the strength to leave my bedroom, we set up a camera, and did a sample report on, ironically, flu season. We sent it to the producers. And after three painfully long months of waiting, we were chosen as web reporters for the show.

Since then, we have reported from Key West, Santa Monica, Washington DC, Philadelphia, and

time and time again, New York City. We've covered everything from Hurricane Sandy, to autism, to Earth Day, to Robert the Haunted Doll—all right by each other's sides. But mainly, we cover entertainment events, and though I am always thankful to have Hannah with me, nothing is more comforting than seeing her next to me on a sensory-overloaded red carpet.

I don't exactly remember my perception of red carpets before I had ever actually been on one, but I am certain that I didn't envision them as being as nerve-wracking as I've come to know them. For one thing, Hannah and I are almost always the only non-adult human beings in the entire vicinity. Sometimes, it's overwhelming to look around at the other reporters in all their I've Been Doing This For Longer Than You've Been Alive Glory. Aside from that, of course there's always that thing of *Oh no, what if I forget how to talk or think or breathe in the middle of an interview*? These are all fears that just disappear into thin air the second I look at my sister. It goes back to the concept of us living our whole lives together. I see her with her microphone in hand and a goofy smile on her face, and automatically think back three, five, ten years—to before any of this "interviewing" stuff was even a thought.

I remember things like our second-grade homework sessions in the backyard oak tree, our fifth-grade inside jokes, and our seventh-grade school drama, and I just can't be anxious anymore. It puts everything into perspective: no matter where we are or what we are doing, I am only the me I have always been and she is only her. And all we can do is enjoy every second of each opportunity we get. Maybe if I didn't have a twin, I would be nervous about interviewing A-list celebrities despite the fact that I haven't even gotten a journalism degree yet. But seriously, how in the world could I be nervous about doing *anything* when I have my childhood best friend next to me, perpetually ready to make a joke about any one of my apprehensive remarks?

Maybe we weren't right for lacrosse, or any sport for that matter. But now we have our own team, a two-player laughing duo who questions anyone and everyone with an interesting story to tell.

Call us the Twinterviewers.

## The Scooter Twins

*Everyone who knows us* is fully aware that we spend a good bit of our lives out on our neon-colored Go-Peds—me on green, Hannah on pink.

We ride for miles—nonstop—sometimes even when it's pouring down rain or snowing. If we decide that we need to go for one of our scooter rides, we are out the door in seconds, no questions asked.

Here's how we roll.

We drag our Go-Peds across the garage and out the door, hop on, ride side by side down the driveway, and are silent until everyone back home is out of earshot. Then one of us turns to the other, and we just start *talking*.

All of our big decisions, and most of our best ideas, have come from one of our extended scooter rides (or Tours, as we call them).

As we glide through our neighborhood and among the ones surrounding it, Hannah I solve problems, recall memories, and talk about everything that we need to discuss—but also need to be entirely alone for.

I always find myself thinking, *How does this*

*girl understand me so well?* How can two different brains set inside two separate bodies have such a remarkable connection with the other? Hannah just takes the words right out of my mouth. The most astonishing moments, though, are the ones where she starts gushing about something that I had been waiting to bring up, but had been unable to find the words to properly articulate. Likewise, there are times when I have a point to make, and can just tell by the look on her face that she knows *exactly* what I mean. I can't imagine life without a person who understands my mind so well. Maybe it's just me, but I feel like it would be a bit frustrating.

Going back to our duties as The Twinterviewers, I'm sure you can imagine that our lives get kind of insane sometimes—in a good way. We'll go off to New York City and interview people who we've been fans of for years, then stay up most of the night walking around the city, then fall asleep in our hotel room only to wake up again a few hours later. When we travel to work, we barely have time to breathe, much less have personal talks with each other—no matter how much we really want or need to. What I love, though, is that afterwards things always return back to normal. (For a little while, at least, before everything gets crazy again. Not that I'm complaining!) After returning home from one of our adventures, the two of us always go on a scooter

ride right away, and they always start with the exact same sentence: "So, what did you think of all that?"

These are some of my favorite rides. No matter how hectic life can get sometimes, it always becomes serene again after a Scooter Ride Chat with my twin. I'd probably have lost my mind by now if it weren't for them.

Who says scooter rides can't have a dramatically positive effect on the daily lives of teenagers?

## Encourager

*The two of us* are almost never in a bad mood, or in a state where *all* thoughts are negative, at the same time. And thank God for that.

The second Hannah picks up on the fact that I'm feeling down about something, she assumes the role of "encourager." And I do the same for her. So sometimes it's me, and sometimes it's Hannah, but it's strange—I can never tell whether the encourager is actually as optimistic as she appears, or if she is just trying to lighten the mood and bring hope to the situation. When it's me who is trying to cheer up my sister, I find myself spouting every single detail I can dream up of The Brighter Side Of The Situation in an attempt to drill positive vibes into her brain. It's almost like I rely on her reactions to my optimism in order to reassure my own beliefs. Now that I think about it, I'm sure that a lot of it has to do with the fact that in times where I can't even figure out my thoughts and feelings, I find it much more settling to just choose to focus on the good whenever possible. And when I just can't bring myself to put on the rose-colored glasses? That's Hannah's cue to leap into one of her highly enthusiastic speeches of possibly feigned confidence. I can't tell you how many times these conversations have helped us through tough days. And anyway, if you think about it, Hannah and I, or any set of twins for that matter, have a clear advantage in problem-solving. With two minds working on one issue, there is plenty of room for differences in perspective. There's always going to be one of us with a more rational viewpoint, and we each have our own ideas as to how to go about dealing with the same obstacle. Put the two of us together, and we're a Dynamic Dilemma-Solving Duo.

There was one time, however, that Hannah and I experienced a massive disappointment and just kind of allowed ourselves to show it. I'll never forget it, because it was so rare: for once we were dealing with our sadness in an incredibly similar way. I really don't know what got into us and why we both just decided to accept our fate and ride out the gloominess, but it actually felt kind of good to deal with it together. What we were upset about is something that I'd rather not go into detail about, but what stands out to me is the moment that we decided to confront it.

I remember the day very clearly. Hannah and I had just gotten off the airplane after an entire day of travel to, ironically, Paradise Island in the Bahamas, when we received some unexpected bad news. Suddenly even the beaming sun in a cloudless sky didn't feel warm. At first we were both silent, and I recall feeling confused and even a little helpless when Hannah didn't start in with a pep talk. Neither of us uttered a single word on the entire cab ride from the airport to the hotel. We just kind of stared at each other, and I could see the look of defeat in her eyes. After a couple of minutes, I suggested that we go down to the hotel Jacuzzi to take our minds off of the situation, and the two of us began our way down the hallway and into the elevator, dragging our feet and staring straight ahead, still saying absolutely nothing.

It was a heavy silence, which wasn't broken until we got to the pool area and began to climb into the warm water. Just as my toes broke the water's surface, Hannah stopped on the top step and looked me directly in the eyes.

"You know, I can tell we feel the *exact* same

way right now. I can tell by the way you're moving."

By now you won't be surprised to hear that I had just been thinking the same exact thing about her.

And right away, Hannah and I just started pouring all of our emotions out for each other to see. It was strange to be in a situation for the first time where neither of us could find the strength to encourage the other—we could only talk through how we were feeling. By the end of the conversation, all we had come up with was that sometimes bad things happen and you just have to deal with it. Hannah stepped out of the Jacuzzi and draped a towel around her shoulders.

"Come on. We're on Paradise Freaking Island, the *least* we can do is go get some ice cream or something."

Despite still feeling heavy and sad, somehow I went to sleep that night with a slight smile on my face. Life isn't always easy, that's for sure; but what are you going to do but let it roll on anyway?

And I feel beyond lucky to have my sister with me on the ride.

## Being "The Twins"

**"Does it bother you when people get you mixed up, and forget who is who?"**

*We are asked this* all the time. It actually doesn't bother us as much as you might think it would. I can completely understand how people who don't know us well have trouble telling us apart. If somebody accidentally calls me "Cailin," I don't think twice about it. In fact, I don't even

bother correcting them anymore! Why? Because it shows that they at least tried to make a distinction between the two of us. Even though they didn't get it right, they tried, and that in itself means something to me. At least they didn't just say "Hey, twin!" and leave it at that.

See, what really bothers me is when people who *know* us only refer to Cailin and me as "the twins" or "the Loesch twins" and don't even make an attempt to learn our actual names. Or, even worse, sometimes I feel like people think of us as not only a unit, but as the *same person*. Does that sound a little crazy? Trust me, it has happened and continues to happen all the time.

Now, our twin friends, Abby and Lola, do take it personally when people get their names wrong—which is completely understandable. It's because they feel that being called the wrong name takes away their unique identities. But, of course, everyone has their own way of looking at things. And though Cailin and I always have (and always will) be understanding of the people who mistakenly mix us up, or even make innocent jokes about the two of us, there are certainly some instances in which people take things to an all-new level—and maybe a bit too far.

# "The Other One of You"

*Obviously, my family* and close friends see Cailin and me as individuals. They know the subtle differences in our personalities. They know that Cailin's favorite color is blue, while I've always been more of a pink person. They know that I like mint chocolate chip ice cream while Cailin prefers plain chocolate, and they know that Cailin has slightly lighter hair. Well, it's a different story with other people we don't know quite as well. I truly believe they think of us as the same person sometimes, to the point where I actually get *freaked out* to learn that they can tell us apart. This is especially a problem with teachers.

Back in elementary school, I didn't mind being referred to as "one of the twins" or as being one of a pair of "clones." In fact, it wasn't until a few years ago that it bothered me at all. The first time I remember feeling deeply disturbed at the idea that Cailin and I were being viewed as the same person was the December of our eighth-grade year. It was the last day of school before Christmas break, and Cailin and I were in the hallway, cleaning out our lockers.

I quickly thrust an empty water bottle, which had lived on the top shelf of my locker since September, into the trash and slammed my locker door shut. I was in a hurry to get to homeroom, because Mr. P., a firm believer in the holiday spirit, was doing his annual classroom showing of *Home Alone*. I grabbed my unsuspecting sister by the arm and pulled her toward room 215. I was hoping she would get away with watching the movie with my class, because hers wasn't doing anything but sitting around. Miss A. normally let us go to each other's homerooms, but that particular day left no room for taking chances. Cailin couldn't miss *Home Alone*!

I tried to run especially fast when we passed by Cailin's homeroom. I couldn't let Miss A. see that Cailin was sneaking off with me!

"Twins! Hold it right there!"

*Darn it.*

I came to a screeching halt and closed my eyes. When I opened them, none other than Miss A. was standing right in front of me.

Believe it or not, she didn't look mad. Actually, she was smiling! *That's a good sign*, I thought.

She looked us both up and down, as if she were trying to recognize which of us was her homeroom student. Finally, her eyes shot directly at me.

"Cailin!" she said with a half-smile on her face. "Come with me. You can't go with your sister today!"

Like I said earlier, that didn't bother me. So what if she got us mixed up and called me "Cailin"? We do look alike! What happened next is what did it for me.

"Actually, I'm Hannah!" I said to Miss A. I pointed to Cailin. "She's the one you need."

Miss A. rolled her eyes and started cracking up.

"Of *course!*" she said. "I need the *other* Hannah!" She tapped Cailin's shoulder, signaled for her to follow, and then walked away. Cailin gave me this look like she just swallowed a huge pill without water, then slowly turned around and followed Miss A. back to her homeroom.

Now *I* was the one rolling my eyes. So Cailin was "the other Hannah"? And I was "the other Cailin"?

I know Miss A. was just joking, but I didn't think it was funny. Who wants to be referred to as "the other" . . . well . . . anything? She wasn't calling us twins, she was calling us clones—and it felt just as unnatural as it sounds.

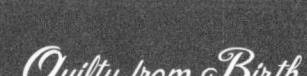

# Guilty from Birth

"*Okay, get into groups* of two and find a spot together. I want you to make a German grocery list that includes prices."

For lots of reasons, Cailin and I love being in the same classes. One big reason is that we work really well together. So, of course, we try to get assigned to the same projects as often as possible. Most teachers don't have a problem with that. As long as we get our assignments done and aren't disruptive, why should they?

On this particular day, we were in German class. As soon as our teacher, Frau W., made the announcement, Cailin stood up and began to make her way over to me.

Across the room, Kate and Riley ran over to each other, sat down, and immediately began laughing about who knows what. Right next to us, Max and Andrew were already loudly rambling on about last weekend's football game. Sara and Kaitlin, best friends since second grade, were practically screaming in excitement about the new *Hunger Games* movie.

Cailin and I, however, sat down and got right to business. That German grocery list wasn't going to write itself!

I was just about to ask her how many Euros she thought broccoli would cost when Frau W. came over.

"Oh, no, no, no. Double Trouble can't work together!"

*Seriously?* She wasn't saying this because we were causing trouble, because we weren't. She wasn't even saying this because she wanted the class to work with people they didn't know so that they would get to know others better, because *everyone else* could work with whoever they wanted.

But not us. "Double Trouble" couldn't work together, simply because they looked the same.

## *Sharing*

*I remember the day very*, very clearly. I was in seventh grade. It was a Monday afternoon in June, and Cailin and I were in seventh-period art class. The room was buzzing with kids, who were running around gathering paintbrushes, paints, and cups of water. The tables were covered with half-finished watercolor self-portraits. The art teacher, Miss J., was standing in front of the room at the chalkboard, giving a demonstration on how to draw perfectly shaped eyes. Cailin and I were sitting side by side, in our assigned seats, next to our friend Kaylee. I finished the drawing portion of my project, and got up to get a paint set and cup of water. Cailin was already halfway done with her painting.

When I got back to my seat, Cailin and Kaylee were having a heated argument about the laws of gravity. I joined in.

Just as I was about to explain Newton's second law, Miss J. walked up. She peered down at my water cup, and then at my sister's. She looked at me with this "Oh, come *on,* Hannah!" face.

*What could possibly be the problem now?* I thought. Miss J. was always on my case about something.

She just kept staring at me with her chin down, her eyes wide, and a weird smile on her face. I could tell she wasn't going to just walk away anytime soon.

"What is it?" I asked her.

She started howling with laughter, as if it were the funniest question she had ever heard. I looked over to Cailin, and then to Kaylee. They looked just as confused as I felt.

"What is it? What *is it?*" She was literally screaming with laughter. "I'll give you a hint. You should be SHHHHHHH . . . SHHHHHHHHH . . ."

I just kept staring at her. I didn't say anything. She continued.

"SHHHHHHH . . . SHHHHHHHHH . . . SHH-HAAAAAARRRRRIIIIINGGG! You and your twin should be *sharing* paint and water cups!"

I scanned the room. Kaylee wasn't sharing with Rafael. Megan wasn't sharing with Belinda. John wasn't sharing with Mike.

And then it hit me. Miss J. thought Cailin and I should be the only two people in the class to share art supplies, simply because we're twins.

Not because we were using the same colors, or working at the same pace, or anything like that—just because we're twins. Miss J. called me out for some pretty ridiculous things that year, but that was by far the worst.

Both incidents, the "other me" and the "SHH-HHHHAAARING" one, took place years ago.

These days, Cailin and I think of them as nothing more than funny stories. Cailin even has me saved as "The Other Me" in her phone contacts. I guess sometimes you just have to find the humor in situations like that, and thank goodness that has always been our specialty.

# The Academic Race

*I was sitting in* AP psychology class a couple of days ago, looking over a graded quiz I had just been handed back, when a girl who sits in front of me turned around in her desk and asked me a question that I get quite often.

**"Do you two get the same grades?"**

Hannah and I weren't very competitive academically until about middle school. I'm not saying that in elementary school I didn't push myself, because I absolutely did, but I didn't worry about my grades in relation to hers.

In fifth grade, Hannah and I took the same classes with the same teachers, but our schedules worked so that we weren't in the same room at the same time. Hannah had math first, so on the day of a test, I'd always find her in the hall after class to ask her whether the test was easy or difficult. Usually, her assessment of the level of difficulty was a pretty accurate predictor of *both* of our final grades.

That year we had a great teacher and a low workload, so we almost always got "A"s. Strangely, however, I would almost always end up with a 93, while most of the time Hannah would earn a 94.

That *really* bothered me for some reason. It was one little point, but it was the reason that I would dread the day after tests when the teacher handed them all back. Fortunately, since then I've adopted a new (and much more realistic) perspective.

These days, I realize that all I can really do is my personal best, and that I shouldn't worry about whether or not the result matches my sister's. However, there is totally still competition between us—only now, it mostly stems from *other* people's expectations instead of our own. Take last Wednesday's science class for example.

The previous weekend, Hannah and I had sat together for three hours studying for our big chemistry exam on the periodic table. During those three hours, Hannah constantly asked me for help—on almost every single problem she attempted. Of course, I answered every question I could, and by the end of our study session, I was pretty confident that we had both mastered the material. So when test time came on Monday morning, I felt prepared and was sure that I'd ace the test. I felt like this all the way to Wednesday, when our teacher walked around the class handing back the graded tests. He gave me mine. It was a "B+."

"Good job, Twinkie, but your twin over there still did better."

I shot a glare at Hannah, who was holding up a paper with a giant red "A" printed on the top.

After class, I ran up to Hannah and demanded to know how on *earth* she had scored higher than I did. I even checked to make sure she had the correct name on the top of her paper. At first, Hannah just looked away, laughing under her breath. Then she looked at me slyly.

"I guess I'm what they call the Smarter Twin."

Oh, brother.

# *Package Deal*

*Something happened in* our tenth-grade public-speaking class that has really stayed with me. It was a Monday morning, and Mrs. B., our teacher, was going around the room having each student tell the class what she or he did over the weekend. It seemed simple enough.

When it was Cailin's turn, she said, "We went on a bike ride, but had to go home early because I hurt my wrist."

I'll never forget the look on Mrs. B.'s face. It was a strange mix between baffled and downright appalled. *What's the problem?* I wondered. *Hasn't she ever heard of someone going for a weekend bike ride?*

After an awkward silence, Mrs. B. looked at Cailin, and then over at me.

"Why don't you ever say 'I'?" she asked us in a shockingly intense tone. Trust me when I tell you that she wasn't joking. She was completely serious.

Cailin was absolutely silent. Everyone in the room was looking at her with wide eyes.

Then she answered sharply, "I said 'we'

because my sister and I were both on the bike ride together."

It was true, we were both on the bike ride together, but what Mrs. B. said that day was also true: when Cailin was asked what she did over the weekend, she responded not with "I went on a bike ride" but with "We went on a bike ride." And that wasn't the first time she'd done it, either. We both have a tendency to speak of ourselves as a single unit, and it took someone else pointing it out for me to even realize it.

Of course, it makes perfect sense for the two of us to use the pronoun "we" more than we use "I"—after all, we do almost everything together. But still, it really made me think. I guess seeing someone genuinely concerned about it really had an impact on me. For the rest of the school year, we both made a conscious effort to say "I" more often in public-speaking class, and everywhere else, too. Mrs. B. had a good point. Maybe we needed to be a little more independent.

That was Step One of our Twin Transformation.

## Stuck Like Glue

*Nine dresses,* "business casual." Four pairs of shoes. Two huge trunks—mine pink, Cailin's blue.

It was the summer before our senior year of high school, we were going to Boston, and we weren't coming home until we had survived two weeks in college. Yes, college!

Cailin and I had both received acceptance letters for an intensive summer journalism program at Emerson College. The idea of spending fourteen days of our summer solely dedicated to journalism was (to say the least) very exciting to us as aspiring reporters.

Because our parents wanted to scope out the area before they just dropped us off in unfamiliar territory for the first time ever, we showed up in Boston a few days before the start of the program to tour around. Before long, Cailin and I basically had the whole place memorized and felt ready to take on the challenges of navigating a big city on our own.

The day before the start of the program was

July fourth, Independence Day, and we spent that evening with our family seeing the annual fireworks show at the Boston Common. As I watched the sky light up with brilliant sparks of red, white, and blue, I felt just a little bit nervous—I was thinking how the following day would be Cailin's and my first real taste of, yes, independence.

The next day was unseasonably cool, and it felt more like fall than the day after the Fourth of July. Along with our parents, Cailin and I walked from our hotel to the Emerson campus, our pink and blue trunks in tow. I was still nervous, but it was just a small reminder that I was about to do something I'd never done before.

Next thing I knew, the entire campus was buzzing with kids from all different programs: stage design, musical theatre, creative writing, slam poetry, journalism—but they all seemed to have one thing in common. Amongst the sea of goodbyes and well wishes, I couldn't help but notice a general aura of nervousness that was so obvious, I felt like I could reach out and touch it. Other kids were feeling like I was!

Then, at precisely 2:30 PM, everything quieted down. Parents called out their last farewells and were gone in minutes. Cailin and I said goodbye to our mom and dad, who reminded us one more time to have fun and text often. One by one, the other students grabbed their trunks and began dragging them to their dorms. At first, all I could do was watch, almost in awe.

They were completely and utterly alone. In a big city. On a college campus. In an unfamiliar place, swarming with unfamiliar people. I had my sister, but the rest were totally flying solo, without a copilot to talk to or laugh it off with if something went wrong.

As Cailin and I got into the elevator, I started doing some serious thinking. Two of the elevator's walls were mirrors, so it was kind of hard not to notice my reflection—and, more importantly, the reflection of my sister—who was standing right there next to me. I couldn't imagine anything different.

When the doors opened on the twelfth floor, where our room for the next few weeks was waiting for us, I noticed something that was extremely eye-opening to me. Even when Cailin and I are alone among strangers (and, in this case, away from our family), as long as we are together, we're never *really* alone. Sure, we had just been dropped off at a college we had never been to before in a state we had never been to before, but we weren't *alone*—we had each other. While most of the students immediately began scrambling to find someone, anyone, to talk to so they didn't feel quite so solitary, I had my best friend right there, as always.

Within hours, Cailin and I were fast friends with our four roommates and fellow journalism students—Sommar from California, Natalie from Arizona, Estelle from Louisiana, and Sarah from Massachussetts—and for the next two weeks, we were practically inseparable. We pushed through awkward man-on-the-street interviews, nearly-impossible Daily News Quizzes, and late-night study sessions together. I felt lucky to have been put with a group of girls who were so compatible—it was fun doing homework together and going out on cupcake runs after class—but even if I hadn't been so lucky, that would've been okay, too: my sister was there.

Even though this was only a fourteen-day summer program, it really got me thinking about how, in just over a year, it would be Actual College—which is much more of a big deal. The thought of that is scary and exciting and nerve-

wracking and it's currently filed in my brain inside of a folder with a giant question mark on it.

One thing's for sure: if Cailin and I end up going to the same college, I won't have to worry about who my roommate will be. In fact, on the last day of the program, as all six roommates stood in a circle in the main lobby just before going our separate ways, Estelle summed up everything that I had been pondering with one simple, Southern-accented sentence: "You're lucky because y'all will always have each other."

So like most of the millions of eighteen-year-olds who go off to college every fall, I will likely be feeling a bit uneasy when the time comes. But I will not feel alone, because at the end of the day, I never really am.

Hey, one less thing, right?

## Looking Ahead

*It was a chilly October* Friday night, and Hannah and I were at a party. We mixed in with a group of four other girls, half of whom we had just met. Already, the conversation was getting deep.

**"There's no way you two are gonna be able to handle growing apart as you get older."**

That comment hit me like a bus. My mind went into what felt almost like a state of panic, but somehow, my heart remained calm.

Was it true?

Suddenly, my entire life with my sister flashed through my memory at the speed of light. Then I realized: being together was all we had ever known. Sure, there were times that we went a few hours, or days at the most, apart . . . but for the first time in my life it hit me that things weren't going to stay that way.

It wasn't long after that day that suddenly, as if on cue, our relationship was put to the test.

## Apart and Alone

*It started off with* a simple question from our dad.

*"Hey, girls! Want to come with me to a Buckeye game?"*

Well, of course! I had always wanted to go to one for as long as I could remember. Our dad is a very proud Buckeye—for the uninitiated, that means he's an Ohio State University graduate—and talks about the football team whenever there's an opening in a conversation. When he can't actually make it to a game, he watches it on TV and screams so loud that the neighbors complain. When the Buckeyes are losing, Dad even has a foam Buckeye "bad-call brick" to throw at the TV. He owns Buckeye T-shirts, shorts, mugs . . . gosh, even socks!

Maybe having him for a dad makes the rest of the family biased, but the Buckeyes are a pretty big deal in our house. So, of course, Cailin and I both answered with a huge *yes*.

"Great!" Dad replied. "Only . . . there's a catch."

Ugh.

"The reason I'm asking is that PopPop can't make it to the game next week, so he's giving me his ticket. I only have one extra ticket right now, so if you want to go, you'll have to go one at a time: one to next week's game, and I promise I'll take the other a few weeks later."

Cailin and I looked at each other. Going separately? Our jaws dropped.

After hours of arguing over who could go to Ohio with our dad first, I decided to put an end to it right there. I'd had enough of the countless coin flips and games of rock-paper-scissors.

"You know what? Let's make this easy. I'll go second," I said to my dad and Cailin.

Cailin looked shocked, but didn't question me for one second. As long as she got to go first, she didn't know and didn't care why I had made such a decision. To be completely honest, I don't even know why I did. I think I just didn't feel it was worth fighting and arguing over.

You know, Cailin and I were so caught up in who got to go to the game first, at first we didn't even consider the fact that we were each going to be alone. For the first time in our lives, we were going to be in separate states—hours away and a plane ride apart from each other.

It really hit me hard when Cailin and Dad left for the airport without me. Not four minutes into their drive, Cailin was already texting me live updates.

**Hannah! We just arrived at the airport. You should see the guy checking in our luggage! He's soo cute!**

**Hannah! There's a Jamba Juice at this airport!**

And a few hours later:

**Hannah! You should see the car we rented! It goes, like, a thousand miles per hour!**

**Hannah.** ***Hannah!*** **I forgot to tell you! The car is *bright yellow*!**

I could almost hear her voice screaming each text from all the way over in Columbus.

I've got to admit, I loved knowing what was going on. Whenever Cailin went more than fifteen minutes without texting me, I got all stressed out and asked what she was doing. I started panicking when she didn't answer. I had this desperate need to know what was going on at all times, and it was pretty exhausting.

All this was happening the weekend before school started and I hadn't finished my summer reading, so I used that as an excuse to sit up in my room the whole weekend and text Cailin. My mom kept coming in and asking if I wanted to go to the store with her or go out to lunch or something, but I refused. I told her that I had too much homework to do, but I actually spent most of my time texting back and forth with Cailin, who was doing the same thing states away in her Ohio hotel room. She was just as desperate to hear what I was doing at every second of the day—and she was supposed to be spending time with our dad!

Needless to say, we were pretty happy when we were reunited at the airport on Monday afternoon. Neither of us wanted to admit it, but we both knew we were completely lost the whole weekend without each other.

The good news is, when it was my turn to go to the game a few weeks later, I was a little bit more comfortable with the idea of us being apart. I still texted Cailin updates whenever I got the chance, but I did enjoy the football game and spent time exploring Ohio with my dad, too. It was strange being apart from each other; but in a way, I kind of liked the independence.

And that was just my first taste of it.

## Two-lane Road

*"You wanna try driving, Han?"*

I was sitting in the backseat of our mom's car, looking out the window with mascara running down my face. I was crying. We had just taken our permit tests at the DMV, and it was bad news.

But only for me.

I'd walked into the testing room with confidence. With a brain packed with info from a series of online pre-tests, I was sure that I would pass.

Hannah and I had even given each other a pep talk beforehand: "If we fail, it's really no big deal. You can always just retake it!"

Funny, though, how we didn't mention what would happen if we got *different* results.

I'll never forget the moment that I filled in my last answer, a rush of adrenaline storming through my body, and immediately got the result. In the center of the computer screen, it presented itself in an obnoxious, taunting fashion:

YOU FAILED.

Now, I know that for lots of people this message wouldn't really be a big deal. After all, most people fail the first time anyway, and you can take it again as early as the following day.

But I wasn't thinking about any of that. All I could focus on was Hannah. What if *she* passed?

It almost seemed like it would be the end of the world. It's crazy, but the mind of a twin works that way. My brain went right to a state where I could only feel an awful sense of doom. Standing out in the hall, I peered into the testing room, only able to see the back of Hannah's head as she typed away.

I had no way of telling how she was doing.

Now, months later, the moment that followed couldn't be clearer in my memory.

Suddenly, Hannah stood up and briskly began to walk to a row of folding chairs set up in the center of the room. As she assumed her position in the chair on the far right, I noticed a pleased little smile on her face.

That could only mean one thing: she had passed. My heart sank down to my feet as a feeling of pure devastation swamped me.

For me, it wasn't just a failed permit test. It was a painfully honest reminder that twinhood does not guarantee identical success and failures for both Members Of The Set. As we left the DMV with our mom, I couldn't counter the flood of horrible thoughts that filled my mind.

*What if I don't pass the next time I try?*

*What if Hannah passes her license test before I even get my permit?*

*What if I never get my license, and Hannah is the only one of us who ever drives?*

*What if from this day on, for as long as we live, Hannah always remains ahead of me?*

Of course, looking back, I realize that these thoughts were completely irrational. Even *then*, I knew they were. But that doesn't mean that in that moment the feelings weren't real.

What can I say? There's something amazing about the bond that twins share. It's incalculably strong—so strong, that the moment it's threatened, it can turn one of the twins into a total lunatic. On that day, I was cursed by the Broken Twin Bond, and I will always remember how terrible it made me feel.

By the way, I got my permit the very next day.

## Growing Pains

*Not so long ago* I learned that it's possible to be fully aware of something for a long time before it truly hits you. And gosh, did a certain something hit me.

I knew it was going to happen someday. To be specific: I knew it was going to hit me hard the day something huge happened to one of us that simply didn't happen to the other one.

Okay, I'm sixteen years old as I write this, and I do know that I'm not the same person as my sister. However, the idea that we'll soon grow up and lead different lives didn't hit me until very recently.

It really sank in when Cailin and I got cast on a TV show called *Celebrity Ghost Stories*. My sister had the lead role of Cherie, while I only had a supporting role as Cherie's twin sister, Marie.

It was hard, to say the least. I just remember the way I felt when Cailin was going over the script for the first time and I was just sort of in my room having this panic attack. It was partly because I was upset that she got the bigger role (there's that twin competition again), but mostly, it was just the idea that we were being treated as two completely different people for the first time in our lives.

I knew I should go downstairs with the rest of the family and act like it didn't bother me, but I just couldn't. I felt like they wouldn't understand. After all, the feeling was strange even to me—and I was the one experiencing it! I had absolutely no idea what to do. I remember just sitting on my bed crying for hours. I could hear Cailin and our parents down in the basement from all the way upstairs. They were reading through the script with Cailin, laughing and making jokes about the things she had to say and do on the show.

Suddenly, the laughter in the basement stopped, and I heard footsteps coming up the stairs. I could tell they were Cailin's. My door flew open and she ran in, laughing wildly.

"Hannah. *Hannah!* You have to read this! Look at all of these things that are in the script! Can you believe I'm going to have to do all *that?*"

I couldn't handle it. I pushed her out of the room, slammed the door, and locked it.

What really got me was the show's story. It

was absolutely fascinating, and the whole plot was centered on an object that Cailin and I had been interested in for years, a Ouija board. In the story, a girl gets possessed by an evil spirit haunting the board, and eventually turns into a demon. And that girl was my sister. For once, it was not both of us—it was just my sister.

The strange thing is, I *knew* I was being ridiculous. I knew this was just part of life, and that sometimes you have to put up with things you wish you didn't have to. I kept telling myself that sometimes in life you fall down, and just have to get back up again.

*One day,* I convinced myself, *it's going to be the other way around, and Cailin will understand exactly how I felt.*

I had a talk with her about it the next day on a scooter ride.

This was one of our *long* Tours.

I tried to explain to her how I felt about the fact that she had a lead role on the show and I was just kind of playing "the sister." She said that she, too, felt really stressed out about it, but for her it was because she had to film all these scenes without me. This only made me more frustrated. Shouldn't that be a good thing for her? She really didn't get it. I got all upset and yelled at her that she was bragging and took the shortcut home without her.

Looking back, I see where Cailin was coming from, being nervous about filming scenes without me. I would have felt the same way if I were in her position. But I was just too upset to actually think it through, so for the rest of the day, we didn't speak.

It only got harder when I had to sit there on the set and watch Cailin film scenes that I wasn't in. It was just me alone with my thoughts, which were eating at my heart like termites.

"Cailin, we need you in hair and makeup!"

"Cailin, you're needed on set in five minutes."

"All right, Cailin, let's film that scene one more time."

All this was going on with my sister, and I was just sitting there, watching. Staring at the Ouija board Cailin had in her lap, I felt my entire life turn into one big mystery that I had no choice but try to decipher. What lay ahead? And how much of it were Cailin and I going to be together for?

I kind of wanted to just grab that board and ask it some questions myself.

It had always been both of us doing it together. And I'm not talking about just acting gigs—I mean life in general. It didn't even sound right hearing "Cailin" by itself. It had always been "Cailin and Hannah" or "Hannah and Cailin."

I tried to reason with myself.

I knew that it all goes back to the fact that we are twins. If I had an older sister, I assured myself, and she was the one who got the bigger role on a TV show, I wouldn't care as much. I would just assume that they wanted someone closer to her age for the part or someone with her look or personality.

But Cailin and I were the same age, looked the same, and acted almost exactly the same. What was it about Cailin that earned her the bigger part? Was I not good enough? Nobody had ever made such a strong distinction between the two of us.

Off the set, we just kept getting into these fights about it. I didn't think Cailin was handling getting the bigger role appropriately, and she didn't think I was handling her getting it appropriately. I accused her of bragging, she accused me of being jealous. Whenever we thought we were done fighting with each other about it, somebody, like a friend or a teacher, would bring it up and it would start all over again.

Like the time Cailin and I went up to one of our teachers to let her know we would be missing a few days of school to film. She wanted to know about the show and who we played and things like that, so Cailin told her about the episode and her character while I just kind of stood there and silently listened.

Finally the teacher turned to me. "And who do you play?"

"I, uh, well, I play her sister." I couldn't come up with a better answer than that. It was still just such an uncomfortable idea. Cailin had gone on and on about her character and how she went through this crazy transformation throughout the episode and how it was such a fun role to play, and I was reminded all over again that I was just "the sister."

The weird thing is that I let this whole thing about Cailin having a bigger role than me almost completely ruin the entire experience, which could have been really fun. It reminds me of this quote by the writer C. JoyBell C., which I still refer to all the time when I'm having a bad day:

*There is a magnificent, beautiful, wonderful painting in front of you! It is intricate, detailed, a painstaking labor of devotion and love! The colors are like no other, they swim and leap, they trickle and embellish! And yet you choose to fixate your eyes on the small fly which has landed on it! Why do you do such a thing?*

Eventually, I decided to just focus on the role I was given and stop comparing it to Cailin's, and I did end up having fun with it. The funny thing is, my character had an important part in the story, too; but I had chosen to completely ignore that and think of nothing else but the fact that it was a different part, a smaller part, than what Cailin had.

Looking back on it now, I completely understand why I was upset. Change can be hard. And this difficult situation finally made me understand a concept I had never been truly able to wrap my head around: Cailin and I are twins, but we are not the same person. We have different strengths, weaknesses, and ways of going about things, so we will not live the same life forever. And that's a good thing!

I learned a lot from that experience. I always knew that one day, something would happen that would hit us both like a freight train and change our lives as twins forever. This was that moment. Even as a baby, I never actually thought we were the same person. I just didn't see us as *individuals*.

Now I do. It wasn't an easy process, but it had to happen.

And I'm glad it happened in the way that it did.

## Together... In Spirit

*At first, Hannah thought* that it was the easiest thing in the world for me to take on a responsibility that she didn't get the opportunity to. The fact is, my internal experience throughout the whole thing was remarkably similar to Hannah's. We were each fighting our own, life-altering battles. Here's my side of the story.

"Cailin will be playing Cherie Currie—the lead—and Hannah will be playing Marie Currie, a supporting role."

I will *never,* in all my life, forget the way hearing those words made me feel.

Ever since we had first taken up acting for fun, we always auditioned as twins. That time was no different: we walked into the casting office together, performed the same scenes for the casting director, and then walked out, side by side. It never crossed my mind that maybe that particular day would be the start of us doing it differently.

But a few days later, when we were cast, it was very obvious that I had been chosen for the bigger part. It may seem trivial to others, but really, the whole thing had me feeling completely stumped. It was a situation that I'd never even thought of as a possibility.

Suddenly, it hit me: for once in my life, I was going to be *really* different from Hannah. And my worst fears were realized when we *didn't* go over our scripts together, laughing and making jokes about how we were delivering our lines. We *didn't* go on long happy Tours through our neighborhood and beyond, talking a mile a minute and scootering even faster because we were too excited to go slow. We *didn't* stay up all night, sitting cross-legged on the floor and spilling everything that scared us and excited us and made us nervous about the experience.

Instead, we just felt bitter about the news. Not just Hannah, but me, too. I just felt so startled by the concept of being my own person for a change. It truly didn't matter who had the bigger role. It was the fact that we had different parts that threw me off.

Just seeing my name at the top of the cast list on the shooting schedule—and Hannah's further down—sent a chill down my spine. We would shoot on different days and have different makeup and contrasting wardrobes. I would have a responsibility that my sister didn't.

In a desperate attempt to lighten the tense mood that none of us could seem to break, I first tried to find humor in the whole deal. Sitting down in the living room with my family that night as I went over my script, I got the urge to make a sarcastic joke about how I couldn't handle doing anything without my sister and wanted to just call it quits. But then I realized something: this was one situation that represented my whole *life*. To spend our entire existence glued to each other's sides and refusing to experience anything apart would be a complete disaster. It would be like sitting eternally on one side of a magnetic force and being so bound by fear that we'd become unable to reach our fingers out and feel the vibrations of the other side, the independent life. We'd be forever trapped in our Strictly Identical Ways Of Living, and the very thought of that took every sharp-tongued remark I would have made and put it out like a flame. Suddenly, it hit me just how important this experience was. It was too crucial to be made into a joke. It was the first day of the rest of our lives.

It was the first time in the sixteen years I had

lived on planet Earth that I felt, really *felt*, like an individual.

We weren't the same person. We were *not* the same person.

The thought of that sent me into a massive anxiety attack. At first, I couldn't even look at the script because the idea of going to the set without Hannah terrified me so much. I felt completely alone and spent a lot of my time sitting in my room, writing down everything that I was feeling because I didn't know who I could talk to about it. Sure, there was my family, but there is only so much a non-twin can understand about the ridiculously complex emotions that come with being separated from your other half. I'd tried to talk to Hannah, who was clearly upset, assuring her that this was bound to happen at one point and that it was no big deal. I told her that next time it would be her that gets to do something without me, and that we were both going to have to get used to it, but Hannah just didn't want to listen. All I wanted was for her to understand that this was scary for both of us and that we were going to get through it together, but she obviously wasn't up for talking about it. I didn't want Hannah to think I was trying to be a show-off, so I opted to just bottle up all my emotions. It was one of the most difficult things I've ever done.

Before that day, I had never known the feeling of not having someone who was going through my exact situation.

Remember our stories about being separated in various school situations, the weekends that we were apart for individual father-daughter trips to Ohio, and even my failed permit test? Those were unusual experiences for us, but this one? It was life-changing.

I knew that I was going to have to take on the challenge by myself—and thank goodness I did.

That first day, when I filmed the show on my own, was one of the most amazing experiences of my life—and the best part is, it had absolutely nothing to do with the fact that I was going to be on a television show. How wonderful it was to experience the feeling of being Cailin for once—not Hannah and Cailin, not Cailin and Hannah, not "the twins" or the "Loesch girls". . . just *Cailin*. That's what the crew and the rest of the cast called me. That's who I am.

"Push that strand of hair out of your eyes, Cailin."

"Cailin, follow me."

"Are you ready, Cailin?"

Just Cailin.

This went on for twelve hours, and it was terrifying and it was nerve-wracking and it was different. But it was thrilling. Before that day, I didn't know what it was like to just be me. I learned that I could handle being my own person when I needed to.

Of course, I never felt happier than I did when I was finally able to reunite with Hannah and shoot scenes together a few days later.

I'll always remember the final scene we shot together for that episode. My character, Cherie, had finally been freed from a burden that she'd been dealing with throughout the show, and we were filming the moment when her sister (played by Hannah) fell to the floor and held Cherie as she cried with relief. That scene was just so incredibly relevant in that moment: it was almost as if our real-life conflict was coming to a close as our characters' on-screen issues were resolved.

Getting emotional for the cameras that night was one of the easiest things I've ever been asked to do.

Even when the director yelled "Cut" after the

last take, Hannah and I continued to hug each other. Having survived our first major experience apart, we knew that we would each leave the set that day with an all-new perspective on life as twins.

Now, as I relive my memories of that month, I realize that it played out like difficult life experiences often do. They first feel like an impending lifetime of misery, but things always fall into place sooner or later. The trouble is that you never see the light at the end of the tunnel until you're already there.

*At last* everything makes sense.

Yes, we are twins. We were born that way and though it sometimes tests our sanity, it is far more often wonderful.

That was not the last time we'll be faced with a challenge that stems from the fact that we live in the often-complex World Of Twinhood. Not even close. We've dealt with a countless number of these experiences already, and will continue to encounter them all our lives. Author and fellow twin Abigail Pogrebin wrote, "Twinship is just a magnified version of everyone's challenge: individuality." Her words ring true in my brain and sink deep into my heart.

Before we know it, we'll both go off to college. Maybe we'll both be accepted into our dream school and be roommates. Maybe we'll buy houses in the same neighborhood and never be more than a mile apart. We both want to be journalists: maybe we'll work together on the same news network or write for the same magazine.

Or maybe we won't. There's one thing that's certain, though: I'm on Hannah's team and she's on mine, and we are meant to navigate this crazy life together. That's never going to change, no matter *what* we go through. It doesn't matter what we'll be doing in five, ten, fifteen years— we will always have that incredible, adaptable, undeniable bond that's one of the strongest relationships in the world: **The Twin Connection**.

## A Letter from the Authors

Dear Reader,

Hannah here. These pages are filled with all kinds of milestones that can best be explained through stories and anecdotes. Though this book you have in your hands is about life as a twin, the basic outline of everyone's life is the same: there's a beginning, an end, and thousands of moments in between. These moments define who you are, who you will become, and who you have always been and always will be. I hope you've gained a better understanding of what it means to me to be a twin, but at the same time have connected my experiences to your own life.

And now it's me, Cailin.

I can't recall the last time I lived a day of my life without writing about it.

Taking each of my life experiences and arranging them into words that can be reread and remembered whenever I choose has always been just plain exhilarating for me. Whether I am absolutely devastated, or confused, or thrilled, or anything in between, I've always found comfort in being able to pull out my phone or notebook and find a way to get my experiences and the feelings attached in a place where they will stay forever.

Writing has always been something that's personal to me, but every once in a while, I get an idea that for whatever reason, I feel just needs to be shared with others. Every story in this book holds its own place in my heart, but I hope that you'll find something about each of them that you can relate to.

Sincerely yours,

*The Loesch Twins*

# Acknowledgements

To all of the names mentioned in the book. In the story of our lives, you're the Diverse And Always-Interesting Cast Of Characters. Thanks for that.

To every one of our family members. Your endless support is what fuels everything that we do.

To Laurie Newkirk and Al Primo. Thanks for believing in us, and thanks for all of the incredible opportunities you've given us over the last few years.

To Ali Smith. Thank you for bringing our vision for the cover photo to life.

To Lisa Pliscou. Everyone says that the editing process is supposed to be brutal, but that was not our experience. Thanks for using your expertise to help us express our thoughts on paper.

To Nancy Cleary at Wyatt-MacKenzie. To set off in search of a home for your book is daunting. After our very first phone call with you, we knew that we had made the right decision.

And lastly, thank you to all the people who ask us about our twin-ness on a daily basis. This book is for you.

## *More on the Authors...*

After years of producing their own web show, Hannah and Cailin auditioned and became the official web correspondents for *Teen Kids News*, an Emmy award-winning television news show for kids and teens. Their celebrity interviews include Nicolas Cage, Emma Stone, Ryan Reynolds, Heidi Klum, Howard Stern, Amanda Seyfried, Howie Mandel, Al Roker, Colin Farrell, David Copperfield, Mel B, Cody Simpson, and more!

Hannah and Cailin have covered numerous events including Vh1's *Do Something Awards*, Comedy Central's *Night of Too Many Stars*, NBC's *The Celebrity Apprentice*, and NBC's *America's Got Talent,* plus movie premieres including *The Croods, Epic, Turbo,* and *Smurfs 2*.

In addition to covering entertainment news, the Loesch twins blog for *Huffington Post Teen* and have reported on topics such as The Battle of Gettysburg, Autism, and Earth Day.

www.ingramcontent.com/pod-product-compliance
Ingram Content Group UK Ltd.
Pitfield, Milton Keynes, MK11 3LW, UK
UKHW020243240426
12048UKWH00026B/1578